O9-ABE-862

WHO LOGIC

WHAT, HOW & OUTCOME

Copyright © 2019 by Jane L. Evarian

All rights reserved. No part of this publication may be reproduced, distributed or transmitted in any form or by any means, including photocopying, recording, or other electronic or mechanical methods, without the prior written permission of the author, except in the case of brief quotations embodied in critical reviews and certain other noncommercial uses permitted by copyright law.

I consider sharing a picture or short text (less than 200 words) from the book on social media platforms an acceptable noncommercial use. If you share, I would be grateful if you used the #WHO-Logic hashtag when you highlight meaningful segments.

For additional usage permission, please contact:

WHO-Logic LLC
P.O. Box 22024
Lansing, MI 48909

www.WHO-Logic.com

ISBN: 978-0-578-50880-1

WHO LOGIC

WHAT, HOW & OUTCOME

A PRACTICAL & TACTICAL VALUATION TOOL
FOR CAREER MANAGEMENT

JANE L. EVARIAN

FOR ME,

For most of my life I have questioned my value. WHO serves as a liberating tool for me. With WHO Logic I internally value and validate. And I can do that because WHO generates evidence of the value I produce.

FOR YOU,

WHO will help you become and stay market ready and advance your career for a lifetime. Know your value, articulate your value, leverage your value.

I OFFER **WHO.**

TABLE OF CONTENTS

| 1 | THE STORY OF WHO LOGIC... 1

WHAT, HOW & OUTCOME

Welcome to WHO Logic! Your Practical & Tactical Career Management Tool........... 2

The Centerpiece of WHO – What Is This Thing Called Valuation?....................... 4

The Origins of the WHO Valuation Framework 5

| 2 | THE LEARNING RATIONALE & THE IMPORTANT MINDSETS...................... 13

Building a Valuation Mindset – The Learning Rationale 13

Important Mindsets 17

| 3 | GETTING STARTED: THE RESUME 21

The Real Reason to Write a Resume – Building a Valuation Mindset 22

Writing Resume Value Points Using WHO Logic 24

Value Point Practice – Seek, Find & Analyze................................. 27

Hello, Jane T. Avatar! WHO Logic Resume Samples & Exercises................. 28

Some Additional Tips for Resume Development 34

The Big Tip for Resume Development – Alignment Matters...................... 35

| 4 | VALUE PROPOSITION.. 39

Creating the Value Proposition 40

Your Turn to Create a Value Proposition! 43

Value Proposition Development – Exercise 45

| 5 | COVER LETTERS 47

The Cover Letter – Why Should You Write One?.............................. 47

Cover Letters & Jane T. Avatar.. 48

WHO Logic Cover Letter Inventory & Alignment Exercise – Jane T. Avatar 52

| 6 | CONVERSATIONAL PITCH & LINKEDIN DEVELOPMENT...................... 57

Structure of the Pitch Outline 58

Building Jane T. Avatar's Pitch Outline for a Networking Event 61

Additional Reminders & Thoughts Regarding the Conversational Pitch........... 69

Conversational Pitch Outline – Your Turn 69

Pitch Framework – Practice 70

Market Readiness – LinkedIn Headline & Summary........................... 72

| 7 | LAUNCHING INTO THE JOB MARKET...................................... 75

MATCHMAKING YOUR WHOS WITH THEIR WHOS

Job Applications & Matchmaking.. 76

Practice Matchmaking – Steps for Aligning Your WHOs with the Job & Company WHOs...................... 78

WHO Inventory & Alignment Exercise (Matchmaking) 79

| 8 | NETWORKING **81**
FAST NETWORKING AND SLOW & STEADY NETWORKING
Fast Networking & WHO Logic 82
Slow & Steady Networking & WHO Logic 88
Slow & Steady Networking Tips & Reminders 99
The Value of Slow & Steady Networking for Career Exploration 103
Your Turn! Build Your List of Companies, Jobs & People 105

| 9 | INTERVIEW PREPARATION **107**
Interview Purpose 107
Interview Preparation using WHO 108
Interview Preparation Exercise 110
General Interview Question Structure 111
After the Interview 124
Offer Negotiation 126
No Offer – No Worries 129

| 10 | CAREER MANAGEMENT **131**
TO FULLY ENGAGE IN INTERNSHIPS & OTHER APPLIED LEARNING EXPERIENCES
Internships & Other Applied Learning Experiences 131
Valuation Practice – Introduction to the Daily WHO-5, Weekly WHO-15 & Final WHO-30 137
Beyond Your Final Reflection & Assessment Practice Using WHO Logic 142

| 11 | CAREER MANAGEMENT **145**
TO FULLY ENGAGE IN CAREER ADVANCEMENT
Aligning Your Smart Work with Company Strategy 148
Career Advancement Valuation Practice Using WHO Logic 149
Jane T. Avatar's Weekly & Comprehensive WHO Valuation Practice ... 152
Jane T. Avatar's Professional Development Story – 5 Years Later 156
Career Management Partnerships & Accountability 157

| 12 | WHO LOGIC FOR COMPANIES **159**

| 13 | WHO LOGIC FOR LIFE **161**

APPENDIX **163**
REFERENCES & BOOK RECOMMENDATIONS **167**
ACKNOWLEDGMENTS **169**
ABOUT THE AUTHOR **171**

The Story of WHO Logic
What, How & Outcome

"I got the job! I assessed my value, aligned my value and built a value-centered authentic network. I got the job!"

- Jane T. Avatar, *Near future*

"I got the raise and promotion! I worked smart and aligned my projects and tasks with the business unit strategy. I continuously assessed my value. I networked inside my company, articulated and leveraged my value and got the raise and promotion."

- Jane T. Avatar, *18 months later*

"I moved into a leadership role! I worked smart by aligning my projects and tasks with the business unit and company strategy. I continuously assessed my value. I networked inside and outside of my company. I articulated and leveraged my value and was invited into the leadership team at a new company."

- Jane T. Avatar, *3–5 years later*

WELCOME TO WHO LOGIC! YOUR PRACTICAL & TACTICAL CAREER MANAGEMENT TOOL

My intention in writing *WHO Logic* is to help people with a process most of us navigate for a big chunk of life—*career management*. We begin our journey through the voice of our main character, Jane T. Avatar. Jane kick-started the book by sharing a snapshot of her progression from an entry-level position to the tactical attainment of a leadership role. And she's just getting started!

Jane T. Avatar understands that career management, a combination of *market readiness* and *career advancement*, requires more than showing up and working hard. She attributes her advancement to a strategic triad—smart work, valuation, and networking. From the earliest origins of her career, it was the process of valuation that anchored her smart work and her networking practice.

How has Jane become an expert in valuation? She uses WHO Logic, a practical and tactical valuation tool that helps uncover, articulate, and leverage value. This little three-letter acronym has been with Jane T. Avatar since she designed her first resume. WHO Logic is the valuation tool that accompanies her throughout the entire market readiness and career advancement process. Please be introduced to the WHO Valuation Framework:

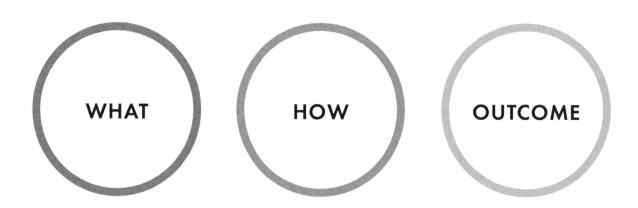

➜ **W** = **WHAT** did you do? *(projects, tasks, initiatives)*

➜ **H** = **HOW** was the work accomplished? *(skills, methods, strategies, technical tools)*

➜ **O** = Intended or Actual **OUTCOME?** *(value, impact, results, scope, learning)*

This book is about uncovering and leveraging ***value***. The goal is to demonstrate how to use WHO Logic as an inquiry and assessment tool, a tool powerful enough to advance your career—at any stage, any level, or any aspiration.

Speaking of value, allow me to share the book's proposition of value, this time using WHO Logic:

The Book's Value Proposition

→ **WHAT WILL THE BOOK DO?** *Help you uncover, articulate, and leverage value*

→ **HOW WILL IT DO THE WORK?** *Using WHO Logic*

→ **OUTCOME?** *To increase your marketability and support your career advancement*

The book will help you uncover, articulate, and leverage value using WHO Logic to increase your marketability and support your career advancement.

WHERE ARE WE HEADED IN THIS BOOK?

We're going to explore WHO! Chapter 1 offers an overview of how WHO originated and evolved. To demonstrate WHO Logic's agility, I will share various uses of the framework in this chapter as a mechanism to warm us up for Chapter 2 and beyond.

Chapter 2 provides the learning and efficiency rationale for WHO. I will also share wisdom from design thinking and several related mindsets, strong influencers of WHO evolution. Chapters 3–11 demonstrate how to use WHO as a valuation tool for market readiness and career advancement.

MY STYLE

Influenced by a lifetime of advising, please know that my writing tone and voice is business casual. I will address you, in the written form, as if we were engaged in a career advising conversation. Please know that throughout the book, I refer to WHO in three ways—*WHO Logic*, the *WHO Valuation Framework,* and *WHO.* The terms are interchangeable and associated with valuation.

WHO IS JANE T. AVATAR AND WHO IS THIS BOOK FOR?

Joining us in the book is *Jane T. Avatar.* Jane has been with me for a long time. Her last name has changed based on the mascot for the university I'm affiliated with, but Jane is like an avatar, which has produced her last name for this book. Her first name is not built from my name, but from the Jane Doe moniker. Jane T. Avatar represents an "every human" moving through market readiness and career advancement activities. (By the way, the T. in Jane's name stands for *The.*)

In this book, Jane T. Avatar is affiliated with a fictional university. She happens to be an undergraduate student enrolled in a marketing program and is an early career professional. I could have selected almost anyone in any profession to serve in this role. I say this because it's possible to think WHO Logic may only be useful for someone studying a certain major, in a specific profession or phase of career. Not the case. I have used WHO Logic with teenage young people as well as polished late-career professionals from a variety of professions, profit and not-for-profit, and at all educational levels.

The point is, the book is about using the WHO Valuation Framework throughout a person's career, regardless of industry or educational level. Let's face it, most of us need to understand, articulate, and leverage our value to advance. This book is for all of us.

THE CENTERPIECE OF WHO — WHAT IS THIS THING CALLED VALUATION?

Value and valuation. Two very important career management terms. Let's start with value and answer the question, **why is value so important?**

Because **value matters**. Almost all decisions we make are connected to value. The products we buy, the experiences we engage in, the relationships we develop, the work we do. Value is measured in nearly every exchange of goods and services.

Value is also deeply associated with *why* companies exist. For-profit companies exist to make money, and this is done by creating value. Not-for-profit companies also exist to create and offer value, typically through advocacy and services.

Supporting the creation of value are employees. Employees represent an investment companies make to generate value from the work that is produced. Employees "sell" their skills and attributes to employers, and in return employers "buy" employees who add to the creation of value. This relationship means that hiring and advancement decisions are value-centric and include **valuation**—the evaluation of someone's potential to add value.

Employers use valuation and so should you. **WHO Logic** is a practical and tactical valuation tool to help you uncover, articulate, and leverage value, a skill you need for lifelong career management.

Valuation is a term most commonly used in finance and accounting and is a process of analysis that generates evidence of worth. According to Investopedia, "Valuation is the process of determining the current worth of an asset or a company."[1]

Valuation is synonymous with any of the following words: evaluation, analysis, interpretation, calculation, assessment, opinion, rating, estimation, or appraisal.

There are several valuation models used in business to assess and articulate value. **WHO is also a valuation model.** *Just like financial valuation, the valuation of You is important.* Regardless of industry or job type, you need to be able to assess your experiences to generate evidence of value.

[1] (Kenton, 2019, p. 1).

TRY WHO LOGIC

I confess, I don't know everything about WHO. I created this valuation framework and am constantly delighted at how I, and others, transform it for career management. Read the book, try the framework. If WHO resonates with you, then incorporate it as you like.

If WHO Logic does stick, consider making it a mindset. What's the *WHO Mindset?* It's often what happens after you use WHO to help build your **market readiness** tools, including resume development, value proposition creation, cover letter writing, networking, interviewing, and offer negotiation. If you diligently use WHO valuation for preparing and updating your market readiness tools, you are regularly analyzing and assessing your experiences, building a valuation mindset along the way. The WHO Mindset is a valuation mindset that can guide your work productivity and career advancement for a lifetime.

WHAT IS MARKET READINESS?

When you are "market ready" you are prepared to promote your value in the job market at any time throughout your career.

What Are Market Readiness Tools?

Anything that provides an opportunity for you to promote your value, including but not limited to the following:

➜ Resumes, Cover & Thank You Letters
➜ Value Proposition & Pitch
➜ LinkedIn Profile
➜ Networking & Interviewing

A WORD ABOUT BALANCE

This book is not about working all the time. It's about understanding your job and aligning your work with the goals and projected outcomes of the organizations you work for, then strategically prioritizing your smart work in alignment with the intended **outcomes**. My intention is for WHO Logic to help you maintain a healthy work life and to do that through consistent valuation.

THE ORIGINS OF THE WHO VALUATION FRAMEWORK

WHO was conceived as a result of observation and empathy. I think students are the best learning lab for anyone who works in education, especially in student services. Students really teach us everything we need to know.

While working at Michigan State University (MSU) in the late 1990s, I discovered that students were struggling with resume writing. Most of the document formatting looked okay or could be easily adjusted; the real challenge for students had to do with evaluating their experiences. These experiences included part-time jobs, internships, volunteering, and campus extracurricular activities.

What I found most often on their resumes were lists of tasks for each experience with no evidence of value. The absence of value-add in a bullet point seemed like a big problem to me, especially since I knew students had rich stories to tell, filled with evidence of value, skills obtained, and lessons learned. But they weren't including these amazing outcomes to articulate value.

Lack of articulating value on a resume wouldn't be a big deal if value weren't considered important, but it is. Employers use resumes to find evidence of value and alignment from past experiences to help predict the value a potential employee can add in the future. I observed that students who were unable to confidently and clearly articulate the value of their experiences were the students often overlooked by employers.

As a result of my observations, I created a valuation framework and shared it with students. The early version of the WHO Valuation Framework wasn't very clever. It was referred to as *TT&A— Task, Tools and Assessment*. Although not very catchy, TT&A worked! Students who used this framework were able to critically think about experiences and articulate outcomes by assessing their experiences. Quite often after using the TT&A framework, they would proclaim a newfound level of confidence in their skills and potential.

I left MSU in 2004 and started working at California State University, Bakersfield (CSUB) early in 2005. TT&A was also used with much success in the Career Education Office at CSUB, but my colleagues and I were soon informed by students that the acronym seemed weird and almost bordered on being inappropriate. I set about renaming the valuation framework, and WHO was born. Just like TT&A, WHO is centered on valuation and offers a more appropriate and memorable acronym.

Here is the original (and still current) WHO resume development framework for analyzing and writing about experiences:

➔ **W** = **WHAT** did you do? *(projects, tasks, initiatives)*

➔ **H** = **HOW** did you do the work? *(skills, methods, strategies, technical tools)*

➔ **O** = **OUTCOME(S)** produced from the work? *(value, impact, results, intention, scope, learning)*

FROM A RESUME-WRITING METHOD TO A COMPREHENSIVE MARKET READINESS VALUATION FRAMEWORK

In the beginning, WHO was exclusively used to help people write value-centered resume statements in alignment with job postings. Applying WHO to other areas of career preparation just happened organically.

BEHAVIORAL INTERVIEW QUESTIONS
Using WHO for interview preparation, particularly for responding to behavioral interview questions, was a logical next step for this nimble framework. It was easy to expand the framework to help individuals respond to the classic behavioral-based question that almost always starts with, "Tell me about a time when…"

Deployment of WHO for Behavioral Interview Questions

Sample Behavioral Question: Tell me about a time you demonstrated leadership within a group of peers?

WHO Framework:

➜ **W** = What was the situation or context?

➜ **H** = **HOW** did you manage the situation? *(skills, strategies, methods, technical tools)*

➜ **O** = Outcome(s) produced. *(value-add, impact, results, learning)*

Behavioral-based interview questions lean on the ***how*** portion of the framework. Certainly, outcomes matter in behavioral interview questions, but it is the *how* in a candidate's response that many employers emphasize.

Again, we return to prediction. Understanding *how* someone managed a previous situation helps an employer better predict future behavior and learn more about relevant skills and qualifications of the candidate. We'll further explore valuation and prediction in the chapter dedicated to interviewing.

WHO EXPANSION
From 2007 to 2013, WHO was primarily used as a tool to help students write evidence-based, outcome-focused, value-centered resumes and as a framework to respond to behavioral-based interview questions. In 2014, WHO grew! Beyond resumes and behavioral-based interview coaching, I started using WHO as a framework to help individuals write cover and thank you letters and as a framework to generate evidence for salary negotiation. I was beginning to see the broader utility of WHO.

I must thank Jessica Best from the University of Oregon for the expansion influence. Jessica is a master career education strategist, and her ability to shape-shift the use of WHO is impressive. She led the charge to incorporate WHO into cover letter writing. Thank you, Jessica!

WHO FOR STRATEGIC PLANNING
From 2009 to the present, the WHO Valuation Framework grew beyond market readiness and nimbly expanded into a framework for strategic planning projects. I discovered that WHO works as an excellent planning tool, a precursor for using WHO Logic to support career advancement practices.

Strategic actions and metrics for business units can be developed easily using WHO Logic. In alignment with the overarching mission and strategy of an organization, the framework looks something like this:

→ **WHAT** will we do? **HOW** will we do the work? What are the intended **OUTCOMES**?

I also used WHO to develop organizational mission statements, which, to me, are essentially propositions of value. To develop a mission statement, the application of WHO Logic looks like this:

→ **WHAT** do we do? **HOW** do we do the work? **OUTCOMES** produced from the work?

It is my opinion that some of the best mission statements are concise and use WHO Logic.

WHO FOR YOUR CORE, YOUR VALUE PROPOSITION (VP)

My favorite application of WHO Logic is for value proposition development. Your VP serves as your personal mission statement. It's at the core of WHO you are. Your VP is what makes you tick, gets you out of bed, centers you. Working on a VP using WHO allows for inquiry, evaluation, and the production of your proposition and promise of value. Here's my value proposition:

Jane Evarian's Value Proposition Using WHO Logic:

→ **W** = **WHAT** do I do? What is my working title? *I am a Career Design Strategist*

→ **H** = **HOW** do I do the work? *I use empathy, creativity, and WHO Logic*

→ **O** = **OUTCOMES** produced? *Help people become market ready and advance professionally*

I am a career design strategist who uses empathy, creativity, and WHO Logic to help people become market ready and advance professionally.

YOUR VALUE + THEIR VALUE (AKA, YOUR WHOS + THEIR WHOS)

In addition to helping you create your proposition of value, WHO can expand as a tool to support your alignment with jobs and companies. For example, if you are casually exploring jobs or engaged in a targeted job search, you can align using WHO.

→ **W** = **WHAT** does the job do? *(job tasks, activities, responsibilities)*

→ **H** = **HOW** does the job get done? *(skills/qualifications needed)*

→ **O** = **OUTCOMES** produced by the job. *(value-add: to the company/your professional growth)*

Once you evaluate and generate a **WHO profile** for the job, ask yourself, "How do the job WHOs *align* with my WHOs?" If you can answer this "alignment" question in advance, you are better able to adjust your resume and better prepared for networking conversations, the job application, and the interview experience. WHO can be used similarly for company and person-of-interest valuation. More on building WHO profiles and alignment later in the book.

WHO IS EVERYWHERE!

A dear friend and colleague of mine, Tammison Smith, said to me not too long ago, "WHO is everywhere!" Tammison made this declaration after using WHO to help a student develop a personal statement for graduate school applications. Here is how Tammison modified WHO Logic to build a framework for designing the personal statement:

Personal Statement Development Using WHO:

→ **W** = **WHAT** is your passion for the subject area? What informs this desire to pursue the degree?

→ **H** = **HOW** will you use your experience and existing knowledge to add value to the learning community?

→ **O** = Intended **OUTCOMES**: What value will you produce as a result of attending graduate school?

Using WHO, the student was able to construct a persuasive document offering her proposition of value by highlighting how she plans to engage in graduate school and WHO she intends to become as a result of the experience.

I happen to agree with Tammison, WHO is everywhere! As humans, we are constantly assessing, interpreting, and appraising. By deploying WHO Logic, we use a mechanism that allows us to uncover evidence-based value in ourselves and alignment with jobs, companies, and other opportunities. And we discover the value in others through outreach and networking. Thank you for sharing your unique use of WHO, Tammison!

FROM MARKET READINESS TO CAREER ADVANCEMENT

If you aren't convinced yet, here's a very simple reason for building a WHO Mindset. At a very basic level, ***work is an exchange of value*** and you will be managing this exchange of value over the course of your career. You will do some work (value) and you will be compensated for the work (value). You can manage your career advancement passively or incorporate a more active WHO Mindset approach.

THE PASSIVE CAREER ADVANCEMENT APPROACH

The passive approach anticipates that the value you produce is readily noticed and rewarded. The process is basically this—your work adds value, your employer carefully evaluates the value and then rewards your efforts. Raises, promotions, and career advancement opportunities come to you by way of *their* careful assessment of your value (fig. 1).

fig. 1 ▼

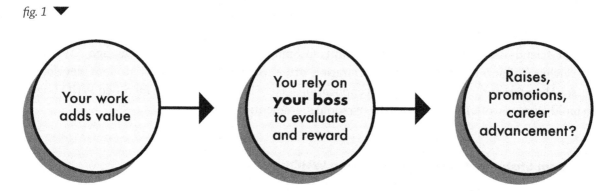

The challenge with the passive career advancement approach is that decision makers aren't necessarily going to carefully assess the value you add. This passive approach places the responsibility on a supervisor while you wait for your value to be carefully measured and rewarded.

THE ACTIVE CAREER ADVANCEMENT APPROACH

Deploying WHO Logic means *you fully engage in valuation* and regularly assess, articulate, and leverage the value of your work. Valuation generates *evidence* that can be used for negotiating salary and opportunities with an existing employer or in the open labor market. By adopting a WHO Mindset, you take an active navigational role in your career progress (fig. 2).

fig. 2 ▼

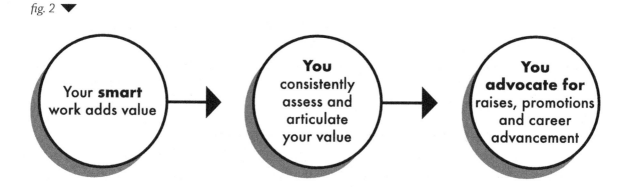

I'm hopeful that by now, you are thinking that using WHO could be an essential tool to help you inventory, assess, and articulate your value throughout your entire career. WHO Logic is nimble and quite simple to learn and use. It's just an inquiry and evaluation framework that, when applied, generates evidence of value.

CHAPTER END & NEXT UP

The first chapter introduced you to the value and broad utility of WHO and provided several examples of how the WHO Valuation Framework can be used. Chapter 2 discusses how the WHO Mindset is developed from the perspective of basic learning principles, and the chapter introduces several influential mindsets for career management.

The remaining chapters represent how to use WHO for the following market readiness and career advancement actions:

→ Personal Branding—*Resume, Value Proposition, Cover Letter, Pitch, LinkedIn*
→ Networking & the Job Search
→ Interviewing & Offer Negotiation
→ On-the-Job Productivity
→ Career Progression & Advancement

Chapter 12 is a short note to employers, encouraging partnership with employees in the career management and valuation journey.

It may be tempting to skip Chapter 2 and move directly to Chapters 3–11, where the practical guidance for using WHO resides. Here's my vote for why you should read Chapter 2: it provides pedagogical evidence that learning one valuation framework is an efficient, simplified, and meaningful approach to career education and management.

The mindsets are also very important. To fully engage in WHO, you will likely need to call on the mindsets mentioned in the chapter. Read Chapter 2. You will learn better, value better, and you may even sleep better. ☺

2

The Learning Rationale & the Important Mindsets

Welcome to Chapter 2! This chapter is a bit bifurcated. If you are a student reading the book, I invite you to read the entire chapter; however, I completely understand if you skip the *Learning Rationale* segment and move directly to the *Important Mindsets* segment.

The *Learning Rationale* segment is primarily speaking to anyone working directly in career services or in related career education roles. I happen to believe that everyone is a career educator, so please know I extend a broad invitation to all readers.

In this chapter I will work to accomplish several goals: (1) provide a learning and efficiency rationale for adopting WHO, and (2) share several mindsets that influence and align with WHO Logic.

BUILDING A VALUATION MINDSET – THE LEARNING RATIONALE

My hope is that my colleagues in career services find this chapter useful, that the goal for deep and sticky learning is shared among all of us working in the field. I'll share what I have come to understand about how learning happens and the rationale for using one framework to build a valuation mindset.

I urge you to consider how the learning process works in relation to the number of existing frameworks available to students—one for resume, another for cover letter writing, something else for interviewing, and the list continues. Too many frameworks can create confusion and make deep, sticky learning difficult to achieve.

Deploying WHO as *the* singular framework to help students with career management means that a valuation mindset is more likely to develop, useful in today's competitive and fast-changing workforce landscape. Using WHO as the singular framework also simplifies and streamlines teaching and learning.

To my career service colleagues, if you don't have an existing career education curriculum, consider developing one using this book as a guide. I am confident that using WHO Logic throughout market readiness and career advancement teachings will result in better learning.

HOW LEARNING HAPPENS

Several years ago, I became very interested in how people learn. I read lots of books and articles and took a course. What I learned about learning, from a rudimentary overview of neuroscience, is that the best way for a concept to stick is by ***introducing*** the concept, ***practicing*** the concept through repetition and recall, then ***elevating*** the practice by adding new and different uses for the concept. The concept "sticks" by moving from short-term or working memory to long-term memory by way of repetition, recall, and elevated use (fig. 3).

fig. 3 ▼

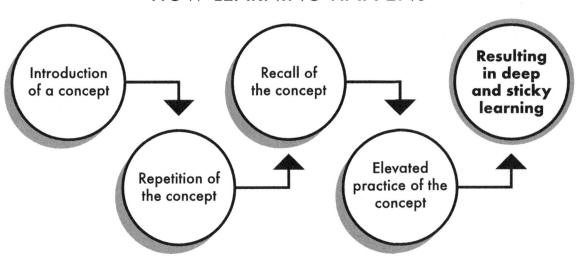

HOW LEARNING HAPPENS

HOW LEARNING WHO HAPPENS

If we apply these fundamental learning principles, WHO Logic strengthens and solidifies with repetition, recall, and elevated use, then moves to long-term memory, where it is available for application at any time. Consistent use may even result in the development of a valuation mindset, the WHO Mindset (fig. 4).

fig. 4 ▶

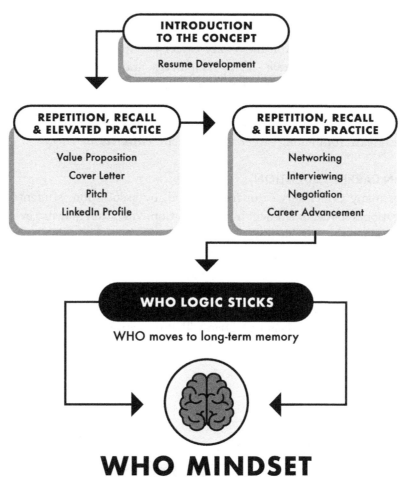

Please allow one more plug for learning! When an individual deploys WHO Logic, the person is reflecting, analyzing, and assessing, important actions for critical thinking and learning. According to Bloom's taxonomy of learning, higher-level learning occurs when an individual analyzes, synthesizes, and evaluates. And, if Fink's taxonomy of learning is consulted, WHO fits in nicely as well. Individuals apply foundational knowledge and connect ideas from elevated practice while also becoming self-directed learners through the process of self-assessment. To learn more about taxonomies of learning, please find resources in the appendix.

WHO OFFERS VALUE THROUGH EFFICIENCY

Okay, so we now know how learning WHO happens. Why does learning WHO matter and what does this have to do with efficiency and value creation?

Using WHO as a singular framework to help individuals uncover, articulate, and leverage value for market readiness and career advancement is new and perhaps a little disruptive. Having worked in university career service operations for the majority of my 30-year career, I am unaware of any career service operation currently using one framework—centered in valuation, intended for market readiness and career advancement—that is useful throughout the entire career life cycle.

I have witnessed a transformation in university career services, with the philosophy gradually moving from a *placement orientation*—bring employers and students together, support the matchmaking, then count the job offers—to an *educational emphasis* focused on teaching students lifelong career management tools and strategies. WHO Logic fits into the new learning paradigm as an efficient framework tying all market readiness tools together, centered in a critically important skill students must learn for lifelong career advancement: ***valuation***.

EXISTING GAP IN CAREER EDUCATION

The challenge for many career service operations and, by association, students, is the lack of access to an educational model or curriculum for valuation. Valuation may not even be part of the conversation. WHO Logic is a nimble framework capable of helping individuals assess value across the entire spectrum of career management.

There are various frameworks (typically identified in acronym format) used for one or two market readiness actions, (e.g., resume writing, behavioral interviewing), but there is no framework spanning the entire career management spectrum. That is, until WHO.

fig. 5 ▶

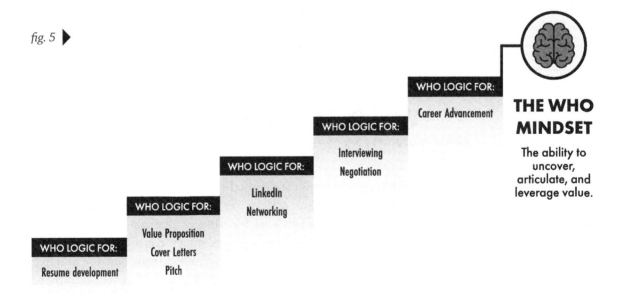

WHO LOGIC FOR:
Resume development

WHO LOGIC FOR:
Value Proposition
Cover Letters
Pitch

WHO LOGIC FOR:
LinkedIn
Networking

WHO LOGIC FOR:
Interviewing
Negotiation

WHO LOGIC FOR:
Career Advancement

THE WHO MINDSET

The ability to uncover, articulate, and leverage value.

WHO FILLS THE GAP

Let's quickly return to how learning happens: a concept is introduced, then repeated and elevated through practice, resulting in deep and sticky learning. Individuals who are introduced to WHO and repeatedly use and elevate the practice of valuation will likely develop a WHO Mindset—a valuation mindset. Figure 5 illustrates this scaffolded iterative process for learning WHO.

Please recall, the reason for using WHO is based on the assertion that work is an exchange of value, and value must be assessed, articulated, and leveraged.

For students, learning and deploying WHO Logic streamlines the market readiness and career advancement process by using one valuation framework to support lifelong career management.

For career service operations, WHO Logic supports the shift from placement to education, offering a nimble inquiry and assessment framework to teach valuation for market readiness and prepare students for career advancement long after they graduate.

I might suggest one of the best ways to teach WHO Logic is to become a WHO Logic organization, one in which team members use WHO to assess and articulate value in alignment with organizational strategy. Additional information and support for becoming a WHO Logic organization can be found in the appendix.

SUGGESTED READING

It is through a basic understanding of learning that WHO Logic has expanded beyond resume development into a comprehensive inquiry and valuation tool for the entire market readiness and career advancement process. If you are a student, educator, lifelong learner, or anyone interested in teaching and learning, I suggest reading *Learning How to Learn: How to succeed in school without spending all your time studying*. Among other work, I have also been influenced by *How Learning Works: Seven research-based principles for smart teaching*.

IMPORTANT MINDSETS

MINDSETS – THE GROWTH MINDSET

WHO Logic aligns quite nicely with several influential paradigms and perspectives. Rooted in positive psychology, Carol Dweck's book *Mindset* is an exemplary work that speaks to the necessity of a growth mindset for personal and professional success. WHO Logic also represents success, using valuation as a mechanism to help you uncover, articulate, and leverage your success.

Applying WHO can be a difficult process if your mindset is fixed. Dweck asserts that many of us have this fixed mindset, which is essentially resistance to growth. Individuals with a fixed mindset are more likely to be uncomfortable with challenge and more apt to steer clear of tasks or activities perceived as difficult or unknown. A person with a fixed mindset can even take a very defiant position when faced with challenge so as not to encounter the possibility of "failure." I use quotation marks around the word *failure* not because I am quoting Dweck, but because I want to point out that failure is widely viewed as negative.

I don't believe in failure. It's taken me a long time to get there, but I don't believe in it. I understand that some failure is truly negative with horrible outcomes. But even the worst failure offers the potential to learn and grow, and as difficult as it can be, value can be found in most failure. Failure is an opportunity to learn. Learning means exploring, and exploring means experiences, and having experiences means you have something to assess and value.

By taking on a growth mindset, one in which you are open to learning, comfortable with not knowing everything, and using curiosity as your "true north," you will be able to fully optimize WHO Logic to assess, articulate, and leverage your experiences.

There are many more reasons why adopting a growth mindset is beneficial. I have found the book *Mindset* to be liberating, transformational, and completely supportive of living life with unfettered curiosity. Please read this remarkable book.

MINDSETS – DESIGN THINKING

Specific work coming from Stanford faculty is compelling and truly influential on what I have been doing with WHO. There is Carol Dweck and her growth mindset work, and then there is the Design School at Stanford.

Not too long ago, Bill Burnett and Dave Evans decided to broadly share their extremely popular Stanford course called Designing Your Life (DYL), and they wrote a book with the same name. I recall sending an email to Bill Burnett with a request for the course syllabus in 2015, and he kindly responded with a note indicating the book was forthcoming.

I was an early adopter of DYL, using the mindsets to support teaching, consulting and advising. I seem to see everything through a WHO lens, and like the growth mindset, design thinking mindsets and practices are in alignment with WHO. Design thinking anchors everything in **empathy**, understanding the needs of the other.

Empathy works nicely with WHO. I often share the following phrase: "WHO is about you, that's WHO!" That's my attempt at a catchy phrase, but I do mean it. From the WHO valuation perspective, you do need to understand your value, and it's always in relation to how your value can add to the needs of the other. All forms of market readiness are about knowing yourself in alignment with the needs of the other—the company, the job. That's empathy. And you need empathy to deploy WHO.

Along with empathy comes **curiosity**. You must be curious to effectively deploy WHO. WHO requires you to curiously explore the value of your experiences, and to use curiosity as a driver for exploring career possibilities and options.

Trying things, or **prototyping**, is also an important mindset. In order to assess, articulate, and leverage experiences, you must *have* experiences. Go ahead, add a new or different task or project that isn't part of your daily work, take some risks in your job, reach out to people you don't know to find out about their jobs. This is a short list of "prototyping" possibilities. All represent experiences you can assess, articulate, and leverage.

You will also need to periodically use **reframing** to shift your thinking. Reframing is very important for WHO valuation. You will sometimes have experiences that are not pleasant or do not feel successful. Reframing can help you find the value in an experience when you otherwise think there is none. I have found that reframing is best in a collaborative setting. We often need help reframing. I regularly help students reframe during advising sessions. They may label an experience negatively and we spend time reframing to get to a place of finding value. This is why **collaboration** is another important mindset for WHO valuation. Sometimes you just need another perspective to help with your valuation.

The most important mindset for WHO, borrowed from design thinking, is to remember **it's a process. Valuation is a lifelong process**, filled with reflection, learning about yourself and others, critically assessing your work, and strategically planning for your future. WHO valuation, a lifelong process, is an efficient framework developed to help you strategically prepare for the labor market and career advancement.

MINDSETS – ENTREPRENEURIAL

The attributes of design thinking and growth mindsets align with entrepreneurial traits and tendencies. Many job postings list *entrepreneurial mindset* as a desirable characteristic. Books, articles, and blog posts speak to the importance of entrepreneurial traits for professional advancement. Thinking and behaving like an entrepreneur on the job implies initiative, action, risk tolerance, creativity, vision, adaptability, decisiveness, and a responsible and responsive ownership mentality. All great traits.

An entrepreneurial mindset is also important for applying and adopting WHO Logic. Thinking and behaving like an entrepreneur to build and manage your career means you will need to take initiative for the valuation experience. Your entrepreneurial project is you, and WHO Logic can help you strategically explore, engage, evaluate, and leverage your experiences.

SUGGESTED READING

There you have it, strengths-based, positive and purposeful mindsets, available to help you with personal and professional development. Please consider spending time with the work produced by Carol Dweck, Bill Burnett, and Dave Evans. Links to learn more about these influential books and authors can be found in the appendix.

CHAPTER END & NEXT UP

YOUR WHO JOURNEY BEGINS. As we close out Chapter 2 and begin the work of learning WHO, I want to reinforce what I have come to understand about this simple valuation framework. WHO is an incredibly nimble tool, useful for almost any sort of professional or personal evaluation as well as strategic planning and productivity. This book is a demonstration of that adaptability and usefulness.

So, I ask you:

→ **WHAT** will you do?
→ **HOW** will you do it?
→ What **OUTCOMES** (value) will you produce?

I invite you to come along on a journey to explore all the great attributes of WHO for YOU.

3

Getting Started: The Resume

Here we are, Chapter 3! This is the point where we dive into the practical and tactical application of WHO Logic. Let the *WHOification* unfold! I know, that's not a word, but I like to play with any and all language that helps build a valuation mindset, the *WHO Mindset*.

On to resumes, where most market readiness and career education starts.

Here's what you can expect from this chapter, lots of hands-on review and activity. Please prepare to come along and play. We will:

- ➜ Identify the real reason to write a resume—building the valuation mindset
- ➜ Shift from writing bullet points to WHO Logic-infused *Value Points*
- ➜ Seek, find, and analyze value points
- ➜ Meet Jane T. Avatar and her before & after WHO Logic resume
- ➜ Explore tips for using WHO Logic to write value points
- ➜ Uncover additional tips for resume development
- ➜ Review the big tip for resumes—*Alignment*

Yep, lots to do here. So, take a breath, focus, and let's go!

THE REAL REASON TO WRITE A RESUME — BUILDING A VALUATION MINDSET!

If you google "why is a resume important," you will find many answers. Results from my Google search mention responses similar to the following:

➜ Provides a summary of one's background
➜ Offers a first impression
➜ Serves as an advertisement
➜ Highlights skills and accomplishments
➜ Represents a person's brand
➜ Is necessary for the job search

Yes, the resume is significant for all reasons mentioned, but the most important thing about a resume is that it initiates the process of assessment and alignment using **valuation**, critically important for two lifelong activities: market readiness and career advancement.

Someone with a **valuation mindset** generates evidence of value by engaging in regular evaluation of work experiences. And the evidence can always be shared and leveraged as needed.

What I'm about to share might seem blasphemous, disrespectful, or just plain irresponsible. I really am amped up about resumes—after all, this is where WHO Logic is typically introduced. Here's the thing, though: *I don't care much about resumes*, not from the perspective of the Google search results.

Resumes continue to be a necessary part of most job application processes. I understand that and accept this reality. However, if all that is happening on your resume is a list of your experiences without evaluation of said experiences, you miss out on the opportunity to develop a valuation mindset, a skill you absolutely need to manage your career for a lifetime.

The resume represents the beginning of a long and fun valuation project, the ongoing valuation of you. By adopting WHO, you can build an ability to use valuation as a mechanism for continuous market readiness and to advance your career. I am making the pitch for using WHO as your framework for inquiry, reflection, and valuation.

RESUMES ARE VERY SUBJECTIVE

Formatting and content vary. Industry expectations also influence resume appearance and content. What one hiring manager or industry prefers, another might not. I can't tell you the number of times someone has come to me and said, "One person told me to write my resume this way, I made the changes and shared with someone else who works in the same industry, and they advised me to do something completely different." Confusing? Yes!

I have found that the best response to the subjectivity is to keep your resume formatting very simple and focus on writing about your experiences. Use WHO Logic to help you with the most important priority, uncovering and articulating value.

You can have a gorgeous resume with lots of graphics and color, but if you aren't sharing the value of your experiences, you really haven't created a strong marketing piece. You need to help the buyer (the company) understand the potential return on their investment.

Focus on the valuation of your experiences, then adjust resume appearance if the industry and jobs you are targeting appreciate creative aesthetics.

COMPANIES SHOP FOR TALENT!

Think about how you shop. You typically buy a product because it will give you value.

Companies use similar decision-making practices. They hire (buy talent) because they have evidence the job candidate will add value.

You are the *seller* and the company is the *buyer*. Think of applying for a job like selling a product. The product you are selling is you—your skills, your competencies, and your potential to add value!

The general resume set-up, including section headings and basic formatting, can be sourced on the internet or from a career services center. I use a very basic business-style format with no template, just a blank Microsoft Word document using very few native layout tools. I keep it simple. The sample resume in this book was created using Word without a template and can be easily replicated.

LOST IN TRANSLATION (A note about applicant tracking software and templates)

There are some very cool templates available from a variety of sources. Take caution with templates, because many companies use applicant tracking software (ATS). ATS systems are sometimes unable to translate graphic nuances or template formatting, meaning that you run the risk of the company missing your value. Simple use of Word, then conversion to PDF, is advised when you apply for jobs using a web-based application process.

If you are sending your resume via email directly to a human, you can typically share a document that incorporates graphics or a template with less risk of translation loss. I happen to like Canva, a graphic design software that is mostly free with some very engaging templates. Use your resources and find something that is reflective of your style and appropriate for your target industry.

WRITING RESUME VALUE POINTS USING WHO LOGIC

Throughout the years I have referred to resumes that incorporate WHO Logic as **evidence-based resumes**. When you use What, How and Outcome logic to assess your experiences, you generate evidence of value, creating what I refer to as **Value Points**.

HOW TO WRITE VALUE POINTS USING WHO

→ Choose **experiences** to include on your resume (your experiences can include jobs, internships, co-op, volunteering, club membership, course projects, research, or study abroad).

→ Choose **tasks** and **projects** from each experience that have the potential to demonstrate value.

→ Evaluate your experiences and tasks by applying **WHO Logic** to help you develop value points.

WHO VALUATION FRAMEWORK (AKA – WHO LOGIC)

→ **W** = **WHAT** did you do? *(projects, tasks, initiatives)*

→ **H** = **HOW** did you do the work? *(skills, methods, strategies, technical tools)*

→ **O** = **OUTCOME(S)** produced from the work? *(value, impact, results, intention, scope, learning)*

WHO Logic in Action. Regardless of where you are in your career—minimal experience, mid-level experience, or very experienced—WHO Logic helps you uncover value. And in the marketplace, the labor market to be exact, hiring and advancement decisions are made based on value.

RESUME VALUE POINT DISSECTION EXERCISE – IDENTIFYING THE VALUE

Let's review two typical experiences, one representing a leadership role (Vini), the other an account management position (Beau). For each experience, you will find a *"Before WHO"* bullet point and an *"After WHO"* value point, along with an analysis of What, How and Outcome.

EXPERIENCE #1: STUDENT CLUB VICE PRESIDENT

This individual serves as the vice president for membership. Let's call her Vini.

Before WHO Logic - Bullet Point:

- Responsible for new member orientation.

After WHO Logic - Value Point:

- Led new member orientation by introducing team-building activities to build affiliation and club loyalty, increased year-end retention by 60% from previous cycle.

> *Vini's role includes responsibility for new member orientation. The before bullet is an example of "stuck in the what." The value of the task is unknown. Vini shares what she does, but the value is unknown without how or outcome.*

WHO LOGIC VALUE POINT DISSECTION:

Leading the new member orientation is the **What**; introducing team-building activities represents **How** the member orientation was led; and there are two outcomes: the intended **Outcome**, to build affiliation and club loyalty, and an actual **Outcome**, the year-end retention increase by 60%.

The value of How:

The reader (i.e., employer) is informed that Vini has leadership experience just through the action verb used to open her value point, and she led the task using team-building activities. By applying WHO Logic, Vini offers specific evidence of important skills: project leadership and the ability to build teams.

The value of Outcome(s):

The reader can see the intended outcome, to build affiliation and club loyalty, and an actual outcome, increased member retention by 60%. An employer can better predict Vini's ability to add value in the future, and because Vini has moved through the process of valuation she can confidently speak to the value added. Everyone wins!

EXPERIENCE #2: ACCOUNT RETENTION SPECIALIST

This individual serves in an account management support role. Let's call him Beau.

Beau's role includes the goal of retaining accounts in a stressful environment. The before bullet is an example of "stuck in the what."

Before WHO Logic - Bullet Point:
- Provided account support in a high-stress environment.

After WHO Logic - Value Point:
- Deployed active listening and a solutions-centered approach to resolve customer concerns while adhering to policies; retained 96% of accounts, 20% higher than company average.

WHO LOGIC VALUE POINT DISSECTION:

Resolving customer concerns is the **What**; deployment of active listening and a solutions-centered approach represents **How** concerns are resolved; and the **Outcome** is the retention of 96% of accounts, 20% higher than company average.

The value of How:
The reader is informed that Beau has active listening and solutions-centered skills. By applying WHO Logic, Beau offers specific evidence of important skills based on experience serving as an account retention specialist.

The value of Outcome(s):
The reader (an employer) can see the outcome, retention of 96% of accounts, 20% higher than company average. An employer can better predict Beau's ability to add value in the future and because Beau has moved through the process of valuation, he can confidently speak to the value added. Everyone wins!

EMPLOYERS CAN GUESS THE WHAT!

Most employers can look at job titles on a resume and accurately guess **What** you did.

Your tasks and projects (What) are important and part of the story, but your leverage in the resume is really about your ability to demonstrate value.

Uncover value by assessing **How** and **Outcome**.

JUST REMEMBER – DON'T GET STUCK IN THE WHAT!

The "Before WHO" bullet points in this exercise are what I call Stuck in the What; there is no How, and there is no Outcome. Without How, and most certainly without Outcome, there is no clear and overt **statement of value**. An employer is not likely to work that hard to find the value.

The responsibility is yours to provide evidence of value. Please recall, the exchange of goods and services is centered in value. If a company isn't convinced of your value, they are less likely to buy.

VALUE POINT PRACTICE – SEEK, FIND & ANALYZE

Time to Practice! Review the "Stuck in the What" bullet points, then find and analyze the WHO Logic value points.

1. Circle and label **WHAT**, **HOW**, and **OUTCOME** for each value point.
2. Analyze the Value of How.
3. Analyze the Value of Outcome.

PRACTICE SET 1:

Before WHO Logic - Bullet Point:
- Managed social media for company.

After WHO Logic - Value Point:
- Built social media presence using coupons and time-sensitive campaigns, increased sales by 25% within 6 months of launch.

Circle and label
What, How,
and Outcome.

The Value of How:

Analyze the Value of How.

The Value of Outcome:

Analyze the
Value of Outcome.

PRACTICE SET 2:

Before WHO Logic - Bullet Point:

- Filled in for supervisor as needed.

◀ The analysis of Practice Sets 1 & 2 can be found in the appendix.

After WHO Logic - Value Point:

- Assumed leadership role during periodic manager absences and ensured uninterrupted store operations for business with $1.2M in annual sales.

◀ Circle and label What, How, and Outcome.

The Value of How:

◀ Analyze the Value of How.

The Value of Outcome:

◀ Analyze the Value of Outcome.

⚙ # HELLO, JANE T. AVATAR!
WHO LOGIC RESUME SAMPLES & EXERCISES

EXERCISE INSTRUCTIONS:

The following pages include three versions of a resume.

Let's pretend you are the hiring manager trying to fill an entry-level marketing position.

Review the resume versions. Don't be fooled by *Before Who, Version 2*. Length of the statement doesn't mean value has been uncovered and articulated.

Carefully review each resume version, then ask yourself which Jane T. Avatar you would like to interview. Why?

Jane T. Avatar

1234 Happy Lane, Any City, YZ 55555 | (555) 555-5555
jane.avatar963@gmail.com | www.linkedin.com/in/jtavatar

OBJECTIVE
Seeking an internship to apply marketing theory and to practice and gain professional skills.

EDUCATION
Great State University   Any City, YZ
Bachelor of Arts, Marketing, GPA: 3.5   May 20XX

EXPERIENCE
Great State University   Any City, YZ
University Guide   08/20XX – Present

- Lead tours and provide information sessions before each tour
- Use social media platforms and send prospective students interesting information
- Connect prospective students to resources
- Attend all weekly team meetings
- Assist with training of new staff

The Village Pub   Any City, YZ
Delivery Driver   09/20XX – 08/20XX

- Delivered food
- Managed social media for restaurant
- Filled in for management as needed

Taco Bell   Other City, YZ
Team Member   01/20XX – 08/20XX

- Waited on customers, sold food and kept restaurant clean
- Trained new hires

ACTIVITIES & SKILLS

Great State University, American Marketing Association, Member, 01/20XX - Present

Great State University, Club Sports – Soccer, Student Coach and Team Captain, 09/20XX - Present

Proficient with Canva, Tableau, InDesign and Google Analytics

◀ **Version 2** *represents bullet points that are "stuck in the what." Don't let length of the bullet points lull you into the idea that Jane has created value points. Review version 2 very carefully. Are the statements value points or "stuck in the what" bullet points?*

Jane T. Avatar

1234 Happy Lane, Any City, YZ 55555 | (555) 555-5555
jane.avatar963@gmail.com | www.linkedin.com/in/jtavatar

OBJECTIVE
Seeking an internship to apply marketing theory and to practice and gain professional skills.

EDUCATION
Great State University   Any City, YZ
Bachelor of Arts, Marketing, GPA: 3.5   May 20XX

EXPERIENCE
Great State University   Any City, YZ
University Guide   08/20XX – Present

- Lead tours around the entire campus traveling on bikes and buses and provide information sessions before each tour where discussion occurs with prospective students, parents and interested others.
- Post content on social media platforms for prospective students with different messaging depending on high school graduation date and interest areas.
- Connect prospective students to resources across the entire campus; speak regularly with the housing and recreation services as well as the orientation office.
- Attend all weekly team meetings held for the University Guides.
- Assist with training of new staff including providing campus map tips, list of majors and special programs, historical information about the university and other related information.

The Village Pub   Any City, YZ
Delivery Driver   09/20XX – 08/20XX

- Used company vehicle and delivered food in high traffic areas and across the entire city.
- Managed social media for restaurant on a daily basis, used Facebook, Twitter and Instagram.
- Filled in for management including opening and closing, securing of the cash drawer, clean-up and preparation for the next day.

Taco Bell   Other City, YZ
Team Member   01/20XX – 08/20XX

- Waited on customers, communicated orders and kept restaurant clean, processed cash and credit cards, delivered food quickly and accurately and provided great service.
- Trained new hires and shared restaurant rules and regulations including cleanliness and hygiene policy.

ACTIVITIES & SKILLS
Great State University, American Marketing Association, Member, 01/20XX - Present

Great State University, Club Sports–Soccer, Student Coach and Team Captain, 09/20XX - Present

Proficient with Canva, Tableau, InDesign and Google Analytics

Jane T. Avatar

1234 Happy Lane, Any City, YZ 55555 | (555) 555-5555
jane.avatar963@gmail.com | www.linkedin.com/in/jtavatar

VALUE PROPOSITION

Emerging marketing professional who builds relationships and boosts profit by leveraging collaboration, initiative, communication and technical skills.

EDUCATION

Great State University
Bachelor of Arts, Marketing, GPA: 3.5

Any City, YZ
May 20XX

EXPERIENCE

Great State University
University Guide

Any City, YZ
08/20XX – Present

- Promote university by communicating history and traditions during tours offered to over 200 prospective students per week.
- Generate content for segmented markets and send 50+ email and social media outreach messages per month to build relationships and convert prospects to applicants.
- Partner with 30+ student affairs units on campus to connect prospective students with available resources, options and opportunities.
- Collaborate within a team-centered environment by regularly contributing in weekly meetings and assisting with training 10 new members each semester.

The Village Pub
Delivery Driver

Any City, YZ
09/20XX – 08/20XX

- Built social media presence using coupons and time-sensitive campaigns, deployed Google Analytics to measure traffic and increased sales by 25% within 6 months of launch.
- Contributed to company profits by safely meeting all driver requirements to deliver food within time guarantee; produced 20% higher gratuity earnings per quarter than average staff member.
- Assumed leadership role during periodic manager absences and ensured uninterrupted store operations for business with $1.2M in annual sales.

Taco Bell
Team Member

Other City, YZ
01/20XX – 08/20XX

- Ranked first in district sales competition using persuasive communication skills and product knowledge to promote specials and combinations; store exceeded targets by 20% each month.
- Demonstrated leadership and team commitment by training over 20 new hires; used collaboration and role-modeling to ensure company standards were met.

ACTIVITIES & SKILLS

Great State University, American Marketing Association, Member, 01/20XX - Present

Great State University, Club Sports–Soccer, Student Coach and Team Captain, 09/20XX - Present

Proficient with Canva, Tableau, InDesign and Google Analytics

TIPS FOR BUILDING VALUE POINTS USING WHO LOGIC

Influenced by students, WHO Logic evolves, often through direct input from students and colleagues. While teaching students WHO Logic, two of my colleagues, Melanie Butler and Diane Allford, (CSUB), decided to insert helper words such as "by" and "using" for uncovering *How*, **and** they inserted "to" for producing *Outcomes*.

The matrix demonstrates how these helper words serve as prompts for progressing through the logic, helping you find the how and the outcome. Thank you, Melanie and Diane!

WHAT ➝	HOW ➝	OUTCOME ➝	COMPLETED VALUE POINT
List the Task/Project	Insert the words **"by"** or **"using"** to help generate how	Insert the word **"to"** for help generating the outcome(s)	Value Point
Task/Project: Trained new hires	**By/Using:** *Using* leadership *By* role modeling *Using* collaboration	**To:** *To* ensure company standards were met	**Value Point:** *Demonstrated leadership and team commitment by training over 20 new hires; used collaboration and role-modeling to ensure company standards were met.*
Task/Project: Tour prospective students	**By/Using:** *By* communicating history and traditions	**To:** *To* promote university to over 200 students per week	**Value Point:** *Promote university by communicating history and traditions during tours offered to over 200 prospective students per week.*
Task/Project: Assist with training Meet weekly	**By/Using:** *Using* collaboration *By* (offering) regular contributions	**To:** *To* train 10 new members *To* collaborate *To* (offer) regular contributions	**Value Point:** *Collaborate within a team-centered environment by regularly contributing in weekly meetings and assisting with training 10 new members each semester.*

*Note the last example in the matrix. The **How** and **Outcome** are similar. This is common. The point is to discover the **value** of the experience. In this example, **collaboration** and **regular contributions** are identified as valuable attributes to be shared and leveraged.*

YOUR TURN TO CREATE VALUE POINTS USING WHO LOGIC

Select two experiences from your background and generate two value point statements using WHO Logic.

WHO LOGIC VALUE POINT 1:

WHAT ➝	HOW ➝	OUTCOME ➝	COMPLETED VALUE POINT
List the Task/Project	Insert the words **"by"** or **"using"** to help generate how	Insert the word **"to"** for help generating the outcome(s)	Value Point
Task/Project: ➝	*By/Using:* ➝	*To:* ➝	*Value Point:*

WHO LOGIC VALUE POINT 2:

WHAT ➝	HOW ➝	OUTCOME ➝	COMPLETED VALUE POINT
List the Task/Project	Insert the words **"by"** or **"using"** to help generate how	Insert the word **"to"** for help generating the outcome(s)	Value Point
Task/Project: ➝	*By/Using:* ➝	*To:* ➝	*Value Point:*

Deploying WHO Logic uncovers and affirms value. When you assess your experiences using the valuation framework, *What did I do—How did I do the work—What Outcomes did I produce*, an amazing thing happens! Skills pop to the surface and outcomes are uncovered through valuation, and you see that you are truly adding value. You discover you are a problem solver, leader, collaborator, innovator and/or influencer, among other traits that contribute to WHO you are and your proposition of value.

The WHO Valuation Framework produces the same outcome regardless of career level. As your career progresses, your skills and traits evolve. And the cool thing about using WHO throughout your career is that you will continue to discover and affirm *WHO* you are through valuation.

SOME ADDITIONAL TIPS FOR RESUME DEVELOPMENT

USE ECONOMY AND BREVITY
Aim for each value point to be two lines or less. If you think there is no way to reduce a value point, start with the process of elimination. Remove words and determine if meaning and value remain. Resume writing is not prose, and you can let go of superfluous language. Seek assistance if you need help with end product value points, but do not ignore valuation.

DO NOT USE PRONOUNS
Writing the resume in first person without pronouns is a conventional and long-standing practice. Adhere to this convention.

DON'T GET "STUCK IN THE WHAT"
Recall the Jane T. Avatar "stuck in the what – version 2" resume. The bullet points are long statements of what, without how or outcome. *How* and *Outcome*, particularly *Outcome*, speak to value. Longer bullet points are not necessarily value points. After you create a statement, ask yourself if you can clearly identify the value (the How, Outcome or both). If not, the statement is likely not a value point.

VALUE POINT V. PARAGRAPH
I'm a fan of using bulleted value points, but if you prefer using short paragraphs to write about your experiences, the articulation of value is still very important and WHO will work. Remember, resumes are subjective and receive 5–15 seconds of review. People don't have time to deeply dive into your resume. Make it visually easy for your value to shine.

USE ACTION VERBS
Kick off your value points with action verbs. Google "action verbs for resumes" and you will find many helpful choices to support your statements of value and hook your reader.

LEAD WITH OUTCOME, HOW, OR WHAT

"What, How, and Outcome" is the logic framework to help you find value, but you can switch the order of WHO when you construct your value point. You can lead with an Outcome or How, just be sure you use powerful action verbs.

NUMBERS PROVIDE QUANTITATIVE IMPACT AND SCOPE TO SUPPORT VALUE

When you can, include numbers to provide outcomes. Jane Avatar provides a great example of a quantitative outcome as part of her work as a delivery driver by noting a 25% increase in sales due to her social media efforts.

Jane also uses numbers to provide scope. She works with 200 prospects each week and sends 50+ emails per month. The eye is drawn to numeric representation on the resume, and numbers help a reader understand value through scope and quantitative outputs.

WORK FOR YOUR RESUME

Yeah, this is a big one. I advise you to strategically **seek out opportunities** to enrich your professional portfolio. Spend time understanding the mission, strategic actions, and metrics that define success at your company, and take on (or generate) relevant projects. Add specific value to the bottom line. This approach works for volunteer, internship, and club experiences as well.

USE WHO LOGIC

The valuation practice typically starts with the resume and grows in usefulness for lifelong reflection and assessment, serving as your self-marketing and career advancement tool.

THE BIG TIP FOR RESUME DEVELOPMENT — ALIGNMENT MATTERS

YOUR WHOS, THE JOB WHOS & COMPANY WHOS

Aligning your resume with job postings is important! Employers really do expect *you* to do the work of aligning your skills and experiences with the job they have posted. You must make the connection on your resume.

By applying WHO Logic to the job posting and the company, you will better understand the expectations of the job and the culture of the company, making it easier for you to align your skills and experiences with the job posting.

JOB POSTINGS ARE WISH LISTS
Please note that job postings are wish lists and you don't necessarily need to meet every qualification.

Nonetheless, you do want your relevant skills to be prominent on the resume, particularly if a company is using an ATS system to scan your resume for keywords.

THE WHO ALIGNMENT PROCESS

Review the frameworks below. The WHO framework questions are slightly different for job and company analysis, but we're still looking for value and we're also looking for alignment.

Step 1: Apply WHO Logic to analyze the job description to determine alignment.

→ **WHAT** does the job do? (*job tasks, duties, responsibilities*)

→ **HOW** does the job get done? (*skills, qualifications needed to do the job*)

→ **OUTCOMES** produced by the job? (*value for the company and potential for your professional growth*)

Step 2: Find the alignment. Ask yourself questions, including the following:

→ Do my WHOs and the job WHOs align?

→ Are my experiences and interests in alignment with the job tasks, duties, and responsibilities?

→ Do I have skills that meet the qualifications? ***Be sure to highlight relevant skills on your resume.***

→ Do my resume value points align with the value this role adds to the company? ***Highlight the value points that best align with the job.*** Are my value points for each experience prioritized on my resume (i.e., most relevant value points within an experience listed first)?

Step 3: Apply WHO Logic to help you understand the company culture and proposition of value.

→ **WHAT** does the company do? (*mission, core focus, what is produced*)

→ **HOW** do they do the work? (*values, unique attributes, innovations, strategies*)

→ **OUTCOMES?** (*value-add, deliverables, impact*)

Step 4: Ask yourself questions, including the following:

→ Do my WHOs and the company WHOs align?

→ Are my experiences and interests in alignment with the company culture and proposition of value?

→ Do I share similar values with the company? Consider adding one or more shared values on your resume (e.g., inclusivity, blue sky thinking, curiosity, team approach, empathy, etc.).

→ Do my value points align with the value the company adds? ***Highlight the value points that best align with the company.*** Are they prioritized on your resume (i.e., most relevant value point listed first and so on...)?

Make the WHO alignment activity a regular practice when you apply for jobs. Find the alignment, then sell your value.

CHAPTER END & NEXT UP

There it is, resume development using WHO Logic. The point here is to be sure you fully evaluate your experiences to enable your skills and value to pop to the surface. WHO Logic is a great framework to help you with this process. After all, WHO is the resume about? It's about you, that's WHO!

The more you understand your value, the easier it is for you to relay your value, not only on the resume, but as you will see, in other forms of market readiness. Keep reading and practicing.

Beyond the resume, WHO Logic is used for other forms of personal branding within the array of market readiness tools. We're journeying toward one of my favorite uses of WHO Logic, the development of your value proposition. I happen to believe the value proposition is your anchor for everything.

You probably noticed that Jane T. Avatar's resume includes a value proposition. This is typically generated after all other content is complete on the resume. If you decide to add a value proposition, it's like icing on the cake, the last thing added to the resume after the evaluation of skills and experiences.

Let's learn more about creating the valuation proposition, the coolest and most fun way to use WHO Logic... just my opinion.

4

Value Proposition

Chapter 3 introduced the use of WHO Logic for resumes, and the journey continues into the world of value proposition, one of many market readiness tools that highlight your value. You will notice a slight alteration in WHO Logic inquiry language for value proposition development, but the logic remains the same—*What, How,* and *Outcome.* Be curious. Let the WHO learning process continue, and welcome to Chapter 4!

The **Value Proposition (VP)** is one of my favorite market readiness tools because of the role it plays in all aspects of career management. Your VP is similar to a mission statement. It's what makes you tick and gets you out of bed. Your VP is the overarching summary of your value. It's your thesis statement, your synthesized declaration of value. It's the anchor, the epicenter, the place where you can always return for a powerful reminder or recalibration of who you are.

When you can declare your value with conviction, you emanate confidence. You say to the world, this is me and this is how I add value. And you make this confident declaration based on evidence generated from the WHO valuation process.

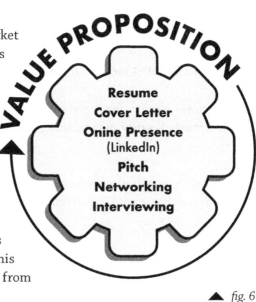

▲ *fig. 6*

Oh, and here's an important note: you should be able to make slight adjustments to your value proposition to align with jobs and companies of interest. Stay true to yourself. The alignment shouldn't be fabricated. Use WHO Logic to produce your authentic value.

You may be wondering, if the VP is at the center, why did we start with the resume? Yep, if I were you, that's the question I would ask.

Here's why: we start with the resume because you need information about yourself to write a value proposition! The resume uses WHO Logic to conduct a comprehensive evaluation of your experiences and generates evidence of your skills and value, providing the information needed to create your value proposition.

CREATING THE VALUE PROPOSITION

Start by considering your working title and where you are headed professionally. Review value points from your resume and highlight dominant skills, methods, technical tools, and other *How-related* attributes. Then consider your most valuable *Outcomes*. Use your analysis and create a comprehensive value proposition. Aim for 30 words or less.

WHAT DOES A VALUE PROPOSITION LOOK LIKE? Please allow me to reintroduce my value proposition using the WHO Valuation Framework.

Jane Evarian's Value Proposition Using WHO Logic:

➜   **W = WHAT** do I do? What is my working title? *I am a Career Design Strategist*

➜   **H = HOW** do I do the work? *I use empathy, creativity, and WHO Logic*

➜   **O = OUTCOMES** produced? *Help people become market ready and advance professionally*

I am a career design strategist who uses empathy, creativity, and WHO Logic to help people become market ready and advance professionally.

If you need to see what informs my value proposition, check out my LinkedIn profile. You should be able to see that my VP is derived from 30 years of experience helping people grow and advance.

YOU NEED CREATIVITY TO GENERATE YOUR VALUE PROPOSITION!

In addition to deploying WHO Logic, you will need to call up a good dose of creativity and a growth mindset to develop your VP. Take a look at your resume. Review your value points. What skills pop to the top? Ask your friends and family what they think are your best attributes. Review job titles of interest. Collect and use data to help you with this project.

DEPLOYING A STEP-BY-STEP APPROACH FOR BUILDING A VALUE PROPOSITION USING THE WHO FRAMEWORK

Think of your value proposition as having three segments: an introduction, a middle, and an end. Each segment links to WHO. The introduction corresponds with *What*, the middle to *How*, and the end is connected to *Outcome*.

Introduction = **WHAT** do you do? What is your working title?

→ Consider your current job title or your status as a student. Think about your aspirational goals and professional direction. Be creative.

Middle = **HOW** have you engaged in work, play, and school? Ask yourself the following questions to help you develop your How.

→ What skills pop from your WHO-influenced resume?

→ What characteristics have you developed based on your experiences and personal values?

→ Align your skills and values with your working title, a job posting, and the career direction in which you are headed.*

End = **OUTCOME** – The outcome connected to What and How.

→ What value have you produced related to your What and How?

→ What impact have you made based on your What and How?

→ What value do you intend to add related to your career direction?

By the way, your value proposition, just like other market readiness tools, evolves based on your experiences and the direction you are headed.

Think of these tools (your resume, value proposition, etc.) as fluid and flexible based on where you have been and where you are going.

*Not sure what skills are needed for the direction you are headed?

Try this! Review 5–10 job postings from Indeed, LinkedIn, or Glassdoor. You will find qualifications listed in the postings to help you align.

You can also google "skills required to be a [fill in a job title]" and you will find plenty of resources.

⚙ FORMING JANE T. AVATAR'S VALUE PROPOSITION

Did you notice Jane T. Avatar's value proposition highlighted on her resume in Chapter 3? If not, return to the resume and look. Let's deploy the WHO valuation framework to formulate her VP.

Introduction = **WHAT** does Jane T. Avatar do? What is her working title?

Introduction/What = **Emerging marketing professional**

◄ *Creatively declares what she does— her working title.*

Middle = **HOW** has Jane T. Avatar engaged in work, play, and school?
→ What skills pop from Jane T. Avatar's WHO-influenced resume?
→ What characteristics has she developed based on experiences and personal values?
→ Align Jane's skills and values with her working title/job posting/ career direction.

Middle/How = **Leverages collaboration, initiative, communication, and technical skills**

◄ *Highlights relevant skills aligned with the direction she is headed.*

End = **OUTCOME** – The outcome connected to What and How.
→ What value has Jane T. Avatar produced related to What and How?
→ What impact has she made based on What and How?
→ What value does she intend to add?

End/Outcome = **Builds relationships and boosts profit**

◄ *Articulates value produced.*

Jane T. Avatar's Value Proposition:
Emerging marketing professional who builds relationships and boosts profit by leveraging collaboration, initiative, communication, and technical skills.

Because of WHO, Jane T. Avatar can provide evidence to prove her value proposition. She is an emerging marketing professional and has leveraged collaboration, initiative, communication, and technical skills to build relationships while working as a University Guide; and she demonstrates the ability to boost profit as a result of her time working for the Village Pub and Taco Bell.

YOUR TURN TO CREATE A VALUE PROPOSITION!

When I help people uncover and write their value propositions, I often start with the creation of a value proposition for a generic product to get some creativity sparking and to help WHO Logic take hold. This is a fun activity and prepares you for generative WHO Logic output. I typically facilitate this activity in groups, so consider grabbing some colleagues or friends to help you get started with VP development.

VALUE PROPOSITION DEVELOPMENT WITH GENERIC PRODUCTS

Select one product from the options provided in the picture. Use the WHO Valuation Framework to create a value proposition for your product. Have fun, be creative. It's actually okay if you're a bit goofy. Just be sure to use WHO Logic.

◀ Do you need inspiration? Skip ahead to the value proposition for Daytona Beach Hands on the next page, then return and create a VP for your generic product.

WHAT *is your product's working title?*

_____

HOW *does this product do the work?* ***Using/By:***

_____

OUTCOME *produced by this product?* ***To:***

_____

Putting it all together. In 30 words or less, share the value proposition for your product.

_____

_____

_____

Sample Value Proposition – Generic Product

WHAT *is your product's working title?*

→ **Daytona Beach Hands**

HOW *does this product do the work?*

→ *Using* **time-released hyaluronic acid and innovative heating particles**

OUTCOME *(value) produced by this product?*

→ *To* **keep hands warm, wrinkle free, and beautiful**

VALUE PROPOSITION:

→ **Daytona Beach Hands uses time-released hyaluronic acid and innovative heating particles to keep hands warm, wrinkle free, and beautiful.**

BE CREATIVE WITH VALUE PROPOSITIONING!

My brain operates in WHOtown all the time and I play with value proposition development a lot. It's fun and involves the creative side of thinking, which is important to me. Join me! Look around, find products (they are everywhere) and generate value propositions. You can do this anywhere and anytime. If you really want to have fun, play generic product value proposition development with a child. They get it. Have fun!

VALUE PROPOSITION DEVELOPMENT — EXERCISE

We practiced value proposition development with generic products. Let's shift and focus on you. Please recall, value is at the center of all buying and selling. Market readiness means you are preparing to sell a product (you) in the marketplace. You are the seller. The company is the buyer and they are buying talent and potential. Buying decisions are centered around value. So, what's your value proposition?

Use the WHO Valuation Framework to create your value proposition.

Introduction = **WHAT** *do you do? What is your working title?*
→ Creatively consider your current job title or status as a student.

WHAT *is your working title?* _____

Middle = **HOW** *have you engaged in work, play, and school?*
→ What skills pop from your WHO-influenced resume?
→ What characteristics have you developed based on experiences and personal values?
→ Align your skills and values with your working title/a job posting/career direction.

◀ *Review a few job postings, identify qualifications and skills required to help you align.*

HOW *do you do the work?* ***Using/By:***

_____

End = **OUTCOME** *– The outcome connected to What and How.*
→ What value have you produced related to What and How?
→ What impact have you made based on What and How?
→ What value do you intend to add related to your career direction?

OUTCOME *produced by you?* ***To:***

_____

Putting it all together. In 30 words or less, share your value proposition.

_____

_____

_____

CHAPTER END & NEXT UP

Value proposition is a very powerful and anchoring force. Your brand starts here, evolves from here, and travels along as you continue to move forward with market readiness and career advancement travels.

We have developed a value-centered resume that captures the direction Jane T. Avatar is headed, and we built out a value proposition for her as well. Jane's value proposition speaks to her overarching value. I'm sure yours does as well!

We'll move forward using WHO Logic for developing value-centered job-aligned cover letters. Jane T. Avatar has identified a job of interest, and she's moving forward to build a deeply aligned cover letter. She's narrowing her value points and aligning her skills and experiences with the position description. Let's travel along to learn how.

5

Cover Letters

Chapter 3 introduced you to WHO Logic, for building value points on your resume and to help you align your WHOs with job and company WHOs. Chapter 4 focused on value proposition, the summary of your value and the anchor for your other market readiness tools. In Chapter 5 we'll apply WHO Logic to another important market readiness tool, the cover letter.

Ah, the mystery of the cover letter. Google "do I need a cover letter," and you will find a variety of responses. Like many aspects of the job search, there is ambiguity around this topic. Some employers read them, some don't. That's all there is to it. If the application instructions indicate a cover letter is needed, prepare the cover letter.

THE COVER LETTER – WHY SHOULD YOU WRITE ONE?

Here's why I like cover letters. My reasoning has nothing to do with whether the cover letter is required, and everything to do with continued valuation and alignment, two critically important aspects of the market readiness and job application process.

Beyond the resume, creating a cover letter provides you with another opportunity to build a very targeted body of evidence that you are a great fit for the role. ***It's an exercise for you***, as well as for the employer. By writing the cover letter, you spend time ***calling out your value*** in direct alignment with the job, thereby preparing yourself at a deeper level for an interview.

A WELL-WRITTEN COVER LETTER "CALLS OUT" YOUR RELEVANT SKILLS AND EXPERIENCES

The resume is typically broader in scope than the cover letter because it includes all relevant value points for each experience. The cover letter narrows the focus, targets the alignment, and calls out your value, specifically and intentionally. The cover letter allows you to pick the most relevant value points from your resume in **alignment** with the job posting.

If calling out your specific value isn't enough, here's another reason to prepare a cover letter. **Sales**. If I want to sell you a product, do I just show it to you once? A resume often represents a singular look at you. By including a cover letter, you are using another persuasive communication tool to introduce and focus your value through targeted and specific alignment with the job and company.

A NOTE ABOUT PERFECT ALIGNMENT

It rarely happens. I think of job postings like wish lists. The company wants to find candidates who meet all the qualifications, but that doesn't always happen. Some applicants get discouraged if they don't meet every qualification articulated in a job posting. This is normal. You likely won't meet every qualification. That's okay. Highlight your skills that do align with as many qualifications as possible. More alignment is certainly better, but remember the mindsets shared in Chapter 2. If you feel hesitant to apply for a job because you don't meet every qualification, try reframing your thinking. Use your growth mindset and a strengths-based approach to highlight your skills and experiences that do align.

COVER LETTERS – TWO OPTIONS

I offer two options for cover letter development: a narrative version and a value point version. Either version is fine. Both provide the opportunity for you to critically think about your connection and highlight the most relevant value points in alignment with the job and company. Generally, the value point option is used by more experienced individuals, as they typically have many relevant value points due to length of work history.

COVER LETTERS & JANE T. AVATAR

To illustrate cover letter development, we need to call on Jane T. Avatar. She has decided to prepare a cover letter for a marketing internship with UVW Incorporated. It's not required, but she thinks this is a great opportunity to go beyond the resume and specifically call out relevant skills.

Jane will need to **inventory the job posting** by reviewing the job tasks and duties, the required skills and qualifications, and the value of the job for the company. She will then **review her resume** to **find the alignment**. She will take time to match her skills and experiences with the skills and qualifications articulated in the job description.

The next several pages include a cover letter outline to guide Jane's work, the UVW marketing internship job description, and Jane's resume. Please review these documents, then take a close look at how Jane aligns her WHOs with the job and company WHOs using the alignment exercise in this chapter.

COVER LETTER **OUTLINE**

Your Name

Mailing Address (optional) | Phone Number
Email Address | LinkedIn Address

September 16, 20XX

Name, Title (If you are unable to identify the appropriate person, use *Hiring Director*)
Name of Company
Mailing Address
City, State Zip Code

Dear [Name or Hiring Director]:

The Introduction. This portion of the letter indicates why you are writing and why you are interested in the job/company and is used as an initial ***proposition of value*** to engage your reader. (If appropriate, you can mention a meaningful affiliation you have with the company; options include someone working at the company who is an advocate, or a connection made at a networking event.) Include a preview of the value points you are going to highlight.

The Middle – Value Point Story 1. This portion of the letter is also known as *Value Point Story #1* and provides an example or story demonstrating a skill that is ***relevant to the employer.*** You can typically select one of the value points from your resume and generate 3–5 sentences to describe the experience. ***Apply WHO Logic to help you fully develop the story.***

The Middle – Value Point Story 2. This portion of the letter is also known as *Value Point Story #2* and provides an example or story demonstrating a skill that is ***relevant to the employer.*** You can select one of the value points from your resume and generate 3–5 sentences to describe the experience. ***Apply WHO Logic to help you fully develop the story.***

The Closing. This portion of the letter makes a clear and concise statement about how your value and alignment relate to the job and company. Make it easy for the reader to connect the dots between what you offer and the work they need you to do. The closing creates an opportunity for you to assertively share next steps, follow-up, or expectations. You can also thank the reader for taking time to review your resume.

Sincerely,

Your Name

MARKETING INTERNSHIP
UVW Corporation (A training and staffing firm)

This 12-week paid internship offers an opportunity for you to work with full-time marketing associates on meaningful projects and contribute to marketing strategy at UVW. A hands-on experience where you will be supported by team and individual mentorship, including regular interaction with senior executives. Join our team of more than 15,000 employees in 22 states and four countries, all committed to our mission, values and sustainable business practices. We celebrate curiosity, entrepreneurial thinking, customer-centered actions, innovative technology usage and outcome-driven tenacity.

At UVW, you will receive quality training and the tools you need to excel in your role while building new skills and enhancing existing abilities. We're interested in your future. Come grow with us during the upcoming summer.

Internship responsibilities will vary based on need. Likely projects for the upcoming summer include the following:

- Partner within a team to generate ideas on customer engagement utilizing digital tools
- Connect existing customers with new product promotions to increase sales
- Plan and develop digital marketing collateral
- Analyze data and provide insights and recommendations
- Research new customer segments
- Leadership responsibilities for team projects

Internship Qualifications:

- Pursuing a Bachelor's degree in marketing, communications, advertising, or related field
- Ability to build working knowledge of UVW's portfolio of products
- Strong written and verbal communication skills
- Ability to think and work independently and within a collaborative group setting
- Knowledge of digital marketing and interest in pursuing a career in this area
- Ability to manage and prioritize multiple tasks and deadlines

Jane T. Avatar

1234 Happy Lane, Any City, YZ 55555 | (555) 555-5555

jane.avatar963@gmail.com | www.linkedin.com/in/jtavatar

VALUE PROPOSITION

Emerging marketing professional who builds relationships and boosts profit by leveraging collaboration, initiative, communication and technical skills.

EDUCATION

Great State University   Any City, YZ

Bachelor of Arts, Marketing, GPA: 3.5   May 20XX

EXPERIENCE

Great State University   Any City, YZ

University Guide   08/20XX – Present

- Promote university by communicating history and traditions during tours offered to over 200 prospective students per week.
- Generate content for segmented markets and send 50+ email and social media outreach messages per month to build relationships and convert prospects to applicants.
- Partner with 30+ student affairs units on campus to connect prospective students with available resources, options and opportunities.
- Collaborate within a team-centered environment by regularly contributing in weekly meetings and assisting with training 10 new members each semester.

The Village Pub   Any City, YZ

Delivery Driver   09/20XX – 08/20XX

- Built social media presence using coupons and time-sensitive campaigns, deployed Google Analytics to measure traffic and increased sales by 25% within 6 months of launch.
- Contributed to company profits by safely meeting all driver requirements to deliver food within time guarantee; produced 20% higher gratuity earnings per quarter than average staff member.
- Assumed leadership role during periodic manager absences and ensured uninterrupted store operations for business with $1.2M in annual sales.

Taco Bell   Other City, YZ

Team Member   01/20XX – 08/20XX

- Ranked first in district sales competition using persuasive communication skills and product knowledge to promote specials and combinations; store exceeded targets by 20% each month.
- Demonstrated leadership and team commitment by training over 20 new hires; used collaboration and role-modeling to ensure company standards were met.

ACTIVITIES & SKILLS

Great State University, American Marketing Association, Member, 01/20XX - Present

Great State University, Club Sports–Soccer, Student Coach and Team Captain, 09/20XX - Present

Proficient with Canva, Tableau, InDesign and Google Analytics

WHO LOGIC COVER LETTER INVENTORY & ALIGNMENT EXERCISE – JANE T. AVATAR

I recommend using the inventory and alignment exercise as a regular practice when applying for jobs. Your goal with this two-step process is to align your skills, experiences, and interests with the job and company.

Please review the steps Jane follows to inventory and align her skills and experiences with the job and company.

Step 1: Inventory: Review the UVW marketing internship job posting. Move horizontally in the table and inventory the job and company using WHO Logic. You may have to deduce the Outcomes from the What and How.

Step 2: Alignment: Review Jane's resume. List relevant experiences, skills, and outcomes that align with the job and company.

◀ *Note that in the real world you would likely have much more data about the company and job, typically found on the company website and related sources.*

INVENTORY		
What does the company do? **What** does the job do? *(List responsibilities, tasks, duties)*	**How** does the company do the work? *(values, innovations, unique differentiators)* **How** does the job get done? *(required skills, qualifications)*	**Outcomes** produced by the company and job?
Company: Staffing firm. Expanding into training and development. Leader in staffing. Locations in 22 states, 4 countries. Job: Generate ideas for customer engagement; connect existing customers with new products; plan/develop new digital marketing collateral; analyze data and insights; research new customer segments; leadership/team projects.	Company: Curiosity, entrepreneurial thinking, outcomes driven, innovative tech usage, customer centered, sustainable biz practices. Job: Pursuing UG in related field; build knowledge of UVW; written and verbal comm; independent & collaborative work; digital mkt knowledge; multitasking skills.	Company: Enhanced leadership positioning, profitability and market share. Job: Contribute to growth in the following areas: customer engagement, new product promotion, marketing collateral development, data analysis and decision making, identification of new customer segments, project leadership.

ALIGNMENT		
Experiences Alignment - What *Jane's Relevant Tasks, Projects*	**Skills Alignment - How** *Jane's Relevant Skills/Experiences*	**Outcomes Alignment** *Jane's Relevant Value*
Most relevant – Expansion of existing and new customers using social media at Village Pub. Digital Marketing – Content generation while working as University Guide & at Village Pub. Leadership while serving as Student Coach/Team Captain, Taco Bell & Village Pub. Communication skills as a University Guide & during Taco Bell experience.	Digital Tools – InDesign, Google Analytics, Tableau, Canva. Content Marketing – generated text and graphics for segmented markets. Social media outreach using FB, Twitter, Instagram. Leadership & Collaboration – Team Captain, Taco Bell trainer. Persuasive Communication – University Guide & Taco Bell – sales.	Increased sales via social media at Village Pub – 25%/6 months. Analytics for decision making. Exceeded sales targets at Taco Bell – 20%. Engage over 200 prospects/week.

Based on the completion of the inventory and alignment exercise, does Jane align with the job and company?

JANE'S COVER LETTER OPTIONS

Jane T. Avatar has generated two cover letters. She used WHO Logic to help her inventory and align and the results can be found on the following pages.

Please review both cover letters.

→ Do you see the results of her alignment efforts?

→ If you were the hiring manager for the internship, would you reach out to Jane to schedule an interview?

→ What version of the cover letter do you prefer?

Jane T. Avatar

1234 Happy Lane, Any City, YZ 55555 | (555) 555-5555
jane.avatar963@gmail.com | www.linkedin.com/in/jtavatar

September 16, 20XX

Hiring Director
UVW Corporation
9876 Happy Blvd.
Happy City, CA 99999

Dear Hiring Director:

I am writing to express interest in the ***Marketing Internship*** with UVW Corporation. I discovered the position on *Handshake* and was encouraged to apply by Sherry Saini, customer experience manager in the Chicago office. I am confident my understanding of digital marketing, combined with leadership and customer engagement abilities align well with the role.

My experiences leveraging social media to drive business have helped prepare me for the marketing position with UVW. For example, while working for the Village Pub, a long-standing local restaurant, I noticed the social media presence was nonexistent. After I shared my knowledge of social media and pitched the power of outreach campaigns, the owner decided to put me in charge of this initiative. I managed the communication plan offering coupons and incentives and utilized Google Analytics to measure traffic. Within six months of launch the restaurant experienced a 25% increase in revenues.

In addition to building a digital media presence for the Village Pub, I have further developed my leadership and communication skills by serving as a University Guide at Great State University. On each tour I lead, I make a point of talking with the prospective students and their families to find out the factors that are important to them in making the decision of where to attend college. I use what I learn to tailor my tours to the potential incoming students in front of me and I summarize this information for my peers in our weekly meetings. The data help us identify trends and adjust our tour content to ensure the on-campus experience is positive.

UVW values curiosity, entrepreneurial thinking and the customer experience. I do too. These values align with every position I have held and most certainly guide my direction moving forward. I am ready to grow with UVW, a company that values sustainable business practices and advancement of team members. I welcome an opportunity to interview for the role with UVW and invite you to contact me at (555) 555-5555. I look forward to hearing from you soon.

Sincerely,

Jane T. Avatar

Jane T. Avatar

1234 Happy Lane, Any City, YZ 55555 | (555) 555-5555
jane.avatar963@gmail.com | www.linkedin.com/in/jtavatar

September 16, 20XX

Hiring Director
UVW Corporation
9876 Happy Blvd.
Happy City, CA 99999

Dear Hiring Director:

I am writing to express interest in the **_Marketing Internship_** with UVW Corporation. I discovered the position on _Handshake_ and was encouraged to apply by Sherry Saini, customer experience manager in the Chicago office. I am confident my understanding of digital marketing, combined with leadership and customer engagement abilities align well with the role. Most notably, my abilities and accomplishments include the following:

- **_Digital Marketing_** - Generated content for segmented markets and sent 50+ email and social media outreach messages per month to convert prospects to applicants.

- **_Creative Initiative_** - Built social media presence using coupons and time-sensitive campaigns, deployed Google Analytics to measure traffic and increased sales by 25% within 6 months of launch.

- **_Ability to Leverage Product Knowledge_** - Ranked first in district sales competition using product knowledge to promote specials and meal combinations; store exceeded targets by 20% each month.

- **_Customer Focused_** - Partnered with 30+ student affairs units on campus to connect prospective students with available resources within short turnaround times.

- **_Peer Leader_** - Served as student coach and team captain for club soccer using active listening and persuasive communication to influence and engage team members.

- **_Team-Centered_** - Collaborated within a team-centered environment by regularly contributing in weekly meetings and assisting with training 10 new members each semester.

UVW values curiosity, entrepreneurial thinking and the customer experience. I do too. These values align with every position I have held and most certainly guide my direction moving forward. I am ready to grow with UVW, a company that values sustainable business practices and advancement of team members. I welcome an opportunity to interview for the role with UVW and invite you to contact me at (555) 555-5555. I look forward to hearing from you soon.

Sincerely,

Jane T. Avatar

CHAPTER END & NEXT UP

Whether the cover letter is carefully reviewed by an employer or not, the primary beneficiary of creating the document is you. Applying WHO Logic to the process of preparing your cover letter means you build another layer of evidence beyond the resume, specifically highlighting value points in direct alignment with the job and company.

Once you establish alignment, you can better promote your value and fit when interacting with the company during networking moments, career fairs, and interviews.

Speaking of networking moments and opportunities to connect with employers, our next stop in the market readiness journey is the use of WHO Logic for conversational pitch and LinkedIn profile development.

6

Conversational Pitch & LinkedIn Development

Recall your value proposition from Chapter 4. It is a market readiness tool and serves as an anchor to help develop your pitch and LinkedIn profile. Once again, you will notice slight adjustments in WHO Logic for pitch and LinkedIn profile development. The basic logic, however, remains the same: *What, How, and Outcome*.

What's this thing called pitch? The pitch, or, as I like to call it, the **conversational pitch**, is an expansion of your value proposition. The conversational pitch typically moves beyond a brief summary of your value to a short conversation. The conversational pitch is delivered verbally, focuses on alignment and value, and is often used to help your listener know what you want.

For example, if you want a job at your dream company, you build your pitch to align with the job description as well as the company mission, values, and deliverables. The pitch is about you, that's WHO. It's also about them, that's WHO.

Pitch is used in many settings. I pitch all the time because I like to share my ideas while learning from others. For me, idea sharing typically includes some form of pitch. When I am trying to influence or persuade, I also pitch. Incorporating WHO Logic helps me generate evidence and demonstrate value. Why? Because value matters.

Conventionally, the pitch is delivered at events that involve verbal interaction—events such as career fairs, interviews, company information sessions, and networking moments. Pitch is incorporated into many market readiness forms of communication, including but not limited to resumes, cover letters, interviewing, and salary negotiations.

From the job search perspective, you pitch all the time. Every market readiness tool is a form of pitching. The verbal pitch should first and foremost be understood as a conversation, one that includes preparation as well as improvisation.

The pitch, like the cover letter, is targeted with a strong focus on alignment with the job and company. Here's the difference between the cover letter and the conversational pitch: The cover letter is a written pitch, the conversational pitch is a verbal exchange. It's a live conversation! Have you ever experienced improv theatre or comedy where there is a general outline, but no specific script? That's the conversational pitch.

THE PITCH CHANGES AT A MOMENT'S NOTICE – THINK OF YOUR PITCH MORE LIKE A PITCH OUTLINE

The pitch is adjustable, improvisational, and ever-changing. I'm going to say it again; your pitch is not a memorized script you recite during a communication exchange. The pitch examples in this segment are shared with you to demonstrate an outline, not a static script.

Pitch means you will engage in a reciprocal conversation with another human, and this conversation includes value-centered moments. Here's the thing to note about humans: they think independently, interject their own questions and curiosities, and steer conversations based on their own unique interests. Yep, humans are unpredictable. This is why your pitch is best developed as a basic outline. You will absolutely need to improvise and pivot. How fun is that? It is fun! It's the beauty of communication, moments of unexpected surprises with opportunity to share, learn, and grow. You need all the mindsets described in Chapter 2 for pitch. You also need the ability to shift and ad-lib.

STRUCTURE OF THE PITCH OUTLINE

A great pitch is engaging and conversational while offering proof of your ability to add value in alignment with the job and company. Think of your conversational pitch as having three segments: an introduction, a middle, and an end. **WHO helps develop the middle**, the segment focused on alignment and value.

Introduction = *Your Name & Working Title*

➜ Introduce yourself, include your current job title or your status as a student.

➜ Express authentic enthusiasm for meeting this person. Mention your interest in the company and job (if a specific job description is available).

➜ Prep to shift to the middle of your conversation.

WAIT! Remember, this is a conversation. You need to deploy basic conversational etiquette. Be natural, briefly pause throughout to be sure you give the listener moments to respond and fully participate in the exchange.

INTRODUCTION IMPROVISATION: During the introduction, make time for your listener to share their name. Be ready for some "small talk" and chat a bit before moving to the middle.

Middle = *Alignment and Valuation, Use WHO*

➜ **W = *What*** have you done that aligns with the job/company?
(Use an example that aligns with the job/company)

➜ **H = *How*** have you accomplished the work?
(Highlight skills or strategies in alignment with the job/company)

➜ **O = *Outcomes*** – Value you have added.
(In alignment with and relevant to the job/company)

End = *An Ask: Ask to stay connected, request a meeting, ask for the interview (as appropriate)*

➜ Engage in the conversation authentically. Maintain curiosity, ask questions, and focus on the company, the job and the person. Offer value points from your resume that naturally fit into the conversation.

➜ At some point the conversation will end. This is dependent on many factors. If you are at a career fair, be mindful of time if others are waiting. Or, if you are at a networking event and it has officially ended, it's likely time to wind up the conversation.

END NOTE!
Obtain the person's contact information. Many company representatives have stopped carrying or distributing business cards.

Regardless of business card availability, you should suggest connection via LinkedIn. If the person agrees, be sure to obtain the correct spelling of their name and remember the company name.

- → If you are aware of an upcoming interview opportunity and you applied or intend to apply for the job, express your interest in interviewing for the position.

- → Offer thanks for the person's time and request contact information to enable you to build the relationship.

- → If you have somehow just found each other—at an airport, in a restaurant, at a social event, wherever—eventually, like any conversation, it will end. Be aware of the situation, be mindful of the person's time, and watch for cues signaling the conversation is ending. Express thanks for the person's time and request contact information to enable you to build the relationship.

WHAT'S THE POINT OF A CONVERSATIONAL PITCH?

Connection and a lasting impression. Alignment with the job and company along with your proof of value, when confidently and authentically displayed, will leave a great impression. You also want your conversational partner (the listener) to know what it is you want—more information, a job, to build a stronger relationship. Be curious, professional, and polite. Express gratitude. Empathy is key when attempting to connect with someone.

BUILDING JANE T. AVATAR'S PITCH OUTLINE FOR A NETWORKING EVENT

Let's return to Jane T. Avatar and her interest in the marketing internship with UVW Corporation. Jane discovers that UVW will be on campus hosting a networking event. Jane builds her pitch framework, eager to demonstrate alignment with the job and company and provide evidence of value.

JANE T. AVATAR – **PITCH OUTLINE** (Version 1)

Jane prepares a **_written pitch outline_** from which she can improvise during her conversation with a company representative.

INTRO:

Jane: "Hello, I'm Jane Avatar. I am working on an undergraduate degree in marketing and I'm excited you are on campus this evening. I am very interested in the marketing internship with the emphasis on digital marketing at UVW. I have used digital marketing strategies to engage customers for most of my jobs. I am confident my skills and experiences are a great fit. Here is a copy of my resume."

MIDDLE:

Jane: "I know that UVW values entrepreneurial thinking and innovative technology usage. I do, too! I really enjoy engaging existing and prospective customers using digital outreach. While working for a small local restaurant, I noticed the social media presence was nonexistent. After I shared my knowledge of social media and pitched the power of outreach campaigns, the owner decided to put me in charge of this initiative. I managed the Facebook and Twitter communication plan offering coupons and incentives and utilized Google Analytics to measure traffic. Within six months of launch, the restaurant experienced a 25% increase in revenues. It was an incredibly fun experience and my initiative made it possible to help the company boost profits."

END:

Jane: "I see that several others are waiting to speak with you, so I won't take any more of your time. Thanks again for hosting this event! I enjoyed speaking with you and will most definitely apply for the internship. Can I reach out to you on LinkedIn and request connection?"

THE REAL CONVERSATION – **JANE'S PITCH** *(Version 1)*

We have viewed Jane's pitch outline. Let's move from the outline and take a look at how this conversation could actually play out.

The Scene: Jane's Conversational Pitch, Version 1: An on-campus networking event hosted by UVW with 30 students in attendance and three UVW employees. A short presentation is followed by open networking. Here's Jane interacting with Zunerah Martin, a representative from UVW.

INTRO:

Jane: *"Hello, I'm Jane Avatar. I am working on an undergraduate degree in marketing and I'm excited you are on campus this evening!"*

Response: *"I'm Zunerah Martin. It's great to meet you, Jane. This is my first time on campus and it's great to meet so many interested students."*

Jane: *"Oh, wow! This is your first time on campus. It's a big place. Did you find the building okay?"*

> Jane did not plan on talking about the company representative's first time on campus. Notice how Jane is able to continue the conversation, off script using improvisation.

Response: *"You're right, the campus is huge. I did get a little turned around, but once I activated GPS, I found my way."*

Jane: *"I'm glad you found the spot without difficulty."*

> Jane could continue with an empathetic story about getting lost on campus. She knows a line is forming to talk with Zunerah, so she moves along.

Jane: *"Again, I'm happy you are here because I have been spending quite a bit of time researching UVW and the marketing internship."*

> This sentence represents the launch into the middle: WHO.

MIDDLE *(WHO)*:

Jane: *"Here is a copy of my resume."*

Zunerah glances at the resume for about 10 seconds, looking for relevant highlights.

Response: *"Nice, you have had several jobs that involved using social media tools. That's great! We are really interested in expanding our social media presence."*

Jane: *"I am confident my skills and experiences are a strong fit for the internship. I know UVW values entrepreneurial thinking and innovative technology usage. I do, too! I really enjoy engaging existing and prospective customers using digital outreach. While working for a small local restaurant, I noticed the social media presence was nonexistent. After I shared my knowledge of social media and pitched the power of outreach campaigns, the owner decided to put me in charge of this initiative. I managed the Facebook and Twitter communication plan offering coupons and incentives and utilized Google Analytics to measure traffic. Within six months of launch, the restaurant experienced a 25% increase in revenues. It was an incredibly fun experience and my initiative made it possible to help the company boost profits."*

Jane's WHO-based example.

What = Developed social media presence, **How** = Using Facebook, Twitter, Google Analytics, **Outcome** = Increased revenues.

Jane demonstrates enthusiasm for customer engagement, entrepreneurial thinking and actions, and relevant technical skills. She aligns with the job description and the company values.

Response: *"That's great, Jane. Yes, you're right, we do value entrepreneurial thinking and actions."*

Zunerah points to the Village Pub on Jane's resume.

"So, you were working as a delivery driver and also worked on social media for this restaurant?"

Jane: *"Yes, I have always been really curious! So, when I noticed the restaurant wasn't using any form of social media, I realized this was a chance to take initiative, work with the owner and help out."*

Jane and Zunerah continue to converse. Jane asks questions about the internship application and interview process, and she poses a few more questions about company culture and vision, until she notices a few more students have stayed on after the event to talk with Zunerah. So she politely ends the conversation.

END:

Jane: *"I see that several others are waiting to speak with you, so I won't take any more of your time. Thanks again for hosting this event, Zunerah! I enjoyed speaking with you and will most definitely apply for the internship. Can I reach out to you on LinkedIn and request connection?"*

Response: *"Sure, Jane. Yes, let's stay connected and do let me know if you have any questions. Have a great night."*

ANALYZING JANE T. AVATAR'S PITCH

Since you have been introduced to WHO Logic for the resume, cover letter, and value proposition, you can likely identify WHO Logic in Jane T. Avatar's pitch. Jane uses WHO to align and share her value by offering a relevant example from her experiences.

→ Can you sense the conversational nature of her pitch?
→ Would you want to interview Jane T. Avatar for this internship role?

ANOTHER VERSION OF THE CONVERSATIONAL PITCH

There are many ways to structure a conversational pitch. **Version 1** focused on **Jane's WHO example** as the centerpiece of the conversation. Jane offered value, using an example to demonstrate relevant skills and experiences in alignment with the job and company.

Version 2 takes a slightly different approach for sharing value and alignment. You will see that Jane uses a **UVW WHO example** as the centerpiece for the conversation.

JANE T. AVATAR – **PITCH OUTLINE** (Version 2)

Jane prepares a **written pitch outline** from which she can improvise during her conversation with a company representative.

INTRO:

Jane: *"I'm Jane Avatar. I am working on an undergraduate degree in marketing and I'm excited you are on campus this evening. I have been spending quite a bit of time learning about UVW from your website and press releases. UVW's effort to engage customers is the primary reason I am attracted to the marketing internship and the company."*

MIDDLE *(The Company WHO)*:

Jane: *"The thing that is so appealing about an opportunity to work for **UVW is the customer-centered approach.** I just finished reading a piece in the* Wall Street Journal *about the UVW Business Applications Conference, bringing customers, partners, and company associates together to share and learn with the intention of making the entire UVW community more connected, agile, and successful. This approach is very inspiring to me. I would love to learn more about the conference outcomes and whether UVW will continue this event annually.*

Based on what I am learning, the use of analytics is so important in customer engagement strategy development. I have been using Tableau in my current role as a University Guide at GSU, filtering data to better understand the interests of prospective students. I have also been creating some very cool visualizations to share the data with the entire recruiting team. We use the data to target our engagement efforts with the goal of converting prospects to applicants. It's fun and I'm learning a lot about this very powerful tool."

END *(the same as version 1)*:

Jane: *"I see that several others are waiting to speak with you, so I won't take any more of your time. Thanks again for hosting this event! I enjoyed speaking with you and will most definitely apply for the internship. Can I reach out to you on LinkedIn and request connection?"*

THE REAL CONVERSATION – **JANE'S PITCH** *(Version 2)*

The scene, Version 2: An on-campus networking event hosted by UVW with 30 students in attendance and three UVW employees. A short presentation is followed by networking. Here's Jane interacting with Zunerah Martin, a representative from UVW.

INTRO:

Jane: *"I'm Jane Avatar. I am working on an undergraduate degree in marketing and I'm excited you are on campus this evening."*

Response: *"It's nice to meet you, Jane. I'm Zunerah Martin and I'm with the customer experience group for the company."*

Jane: *"I was hoping I would speak with someone in customer experience, as I have been spending quite a bit of time learning about UVW from your website and press releases. UVW's effort to engage customers is the primary reason I am attracted to the company."*

Response: *"We have been working really hard to provide user-centered products and services that make sense for our target consumers. It's an exciting time to be with the company. Are you considering applying for an internship or a full-time role with UVW?"*

MIDDLE *(The Company WHO):*

Jane: *"I am! I'm a junior right now, so the marketing internship stands out for me. The thing that is so appealing about an opportunity to work for UVW is the **customer-centered approach** you are speaking about. I just finished reading a piece in the* Wall Street Journal *about the UVW Business Applications Conference, bringing customers, partners, and company associates together to share and learn with the intention of making the entire UVW community more connected, agile, and successful. This approach is very inspiring to me. It would be great to learn more about the conference outcomes and whether UVW will continue this event annually."*

Response: *"Yes, the press has been really favorable, and we are learning so much by building a strong ecosystem between all stakeholders. Did you bring your resume today?"*

Jane: *"I did. I would love to hear your comments on my skills and experiences."*

Zunerah quickly reviews the resume.

Response: *"I see you have had experience working closely with customers and using technology to help companies engage with customers. That's an area where we are expanding, doing some very innovative things to form deeper connections and improve sales, using analytics to guide our strategy."*

Jane: *"This is why I'm so interested in UVW. Based on what I am learning, the use of analytics is just so important in strategy development. I have been using Tableau in my current role as a University Guide at GSU, filtering data to better understand the interests of prospective students; and I use Tableau to create very cool visualizations for the entire recruiting team. We use the data to target our engagement efforts with the goal of converting prospects to applicants. It's fun and I'm learning a lot about this very powerful tool."*

Response: *"Wow, Jane, that's impressive. We are also using some very cool analytics tools. Big data is definitely where things are going. Our goal is to know what our customers want before they do!"*

The conversation continues with Jane and Zunerah talking about specific technologies and strategies related to building stronger customer relationships and driving sales.

END *(the same as version 1):*

Jane: *"I see that several others are waiting to speak with you, so I won't take any more of your time. Thanks again for hosting this event, Zunerah! I enjoyed speaking with you and will most definitely apply for the internship. Can I reach out to you on LinkedIn and request connection?"*

Response: *"Sure, Jane. Yes, let's stay connected and do let me know if you have any questions. Have a great night."*

THE CONVENTIONAL "ELEVATOR PITCH" – **PITCH OUTLINE** *(Version 3)*

Sometimes your pitch really is a 30-second declaration of your value. You may find yourself in situations like large career fairs with lines that are 20–50 students deep. There isn't time for much conversation and your listener just needs your quick and concise pitch.

Your 30-second pitch is an extension of your value proposition, with some carefully selected highlights of your experiences and skills, aligned with the company WHOs and, if there is a known job, the job WHOs.

The other reason your pitch is very short could be lack of knowledge about the company. Perhaps this is a company you spotted at a career fair and you didn't prioritize them as a top company, but now you have an opportunity to pitch. This situation calls for the 30-second generic pitch.

30-SECOND PITCH EXAMPLE FROM JANE T. AVATAR:

The scene: A large career fair where Jane has identified a company that is not on her original prioritized list of companies to visit. There is a very short line to speak with the representative.

Jane: *"Hello, I'm Jane Avatar."*

Response: *"Nice to meet you, Jane. I'm Barbara Gilmore. What can I help you with today?"*

Jane: *"Nice to meet you, Barbara. I am working on a Bachelor of Arts in marketing and will finish in a year and a half. I am passionate about using digital tools to enhance the customer experience and I'm eager to work in a strong team environment where innovative marketing practices are created and used to increase customer engagement.*

I offer relevant experience including the development of digital marketing campaigns in the restaurant and higher education space, and I was ranked first in district sales competitions while working in the quick service restaurant industry. My digital marketing skills include the use of InDesign, Tableau, and Google Analytics.

I would love to learn more about the opportunities available in marketing with your company."

Response: *"Great, Jane. Our marketing internship and full-time jobs are all posted on our website. Based on your graduation date, I'm assuming you are interested in an internship?"*

Jane: *"Yes, I'm looking for an internship. Here's a copy of my resume. You can see, most of my experiences have been in customer engagement, service, and sales."*

Response: *"That's great. Let's talk in more detail about the positions we have available."*

The conversation continues with Jane sharing a bit more about her experiences and skills while Barbara takes notes on Jane's resume. The conversation shifts to a natural end with Jane asking Barbara if she would be willing to connect via LinkedIn. Barbara agrees to the connection and provides Jane with a business card.

ADDITIONAL REMINDERS & THOUGHTS REGARDING THE CONVERSATIONAL PITCH

WHO LEADS THE CONVERSATIONAL PITCH?

Based on reviewing the pitch versions, who do you think leads this conversation? You do! You lead because you want something. You want to introduce yourself, share your value, and leave an impression.

This leadership is *not* a one-sided, overbearing manifesto. Imagine, if you will, a dictator, fist-pounding on a podium, making impassioned declarations. Yeah, that's not the conversational pitch.

Your leadership role during the conversational pitch is confident, subtle, and nuanced. You are inviting someone into a reciprocal exchange. You are trying to connect, align, and articulate your value in relation to what your listener values. The conversational pitch takes practice. If there is one mindset that is essential, it's empathy. Your pitch should be other-focused, relevant, and inviting.

THE CONVERSATIONAL PITCH IS IMPROVISATIONAL

The outline gets you prepared and then you just have to be open to the natural flow of a reciprocal exchange. Don't be a bot. Be curious, be professional, and use empathy to connect and align.

CONVERSATIONAL PITCH OUTLINE – YOUR TURN

This chapter provides an opportunity to view Jane T. Avatar pitching. Viewing and practicing are two different things. You must practice your conversational pitch. Practice with colleagues, friends, family, or a mentor. Anyone willing to learn the framework and provide feedback will be helpful.

It's time to practice! To fully engage in this exercise, you will need to **select a job**. Access any job posting system to find a job of interest. **Use your resume** to help you create your conversational pitch outline. **Use WHO Logic** to help you seek alignment and share your value. Remember, this is an *outline*. You will improvise and ad-lib during live moments.

PITCH FRAMEWORK – PRACTICE

Below you will find the framework for the conversational pitch. Please review and use the framework to help you create your pitch outline on the following page.

Introduction = *Your Name & Working Title*

➔ Introduce yourself; include your current job title or your status as a student.

➔ Express authentic enthusiasm for meeting this person. Mention your interest in the company and job.

➔ Prepare to shift to the middle of your conversation.

Middle = *Alignment and Valuation, using* **WHO**

➔ **W** = What have you done that aligns with the job/company? *(Use an example that aligns with the job/company)*

➔ **H** = How have you accomplished the work? *(Highlight skills or strategies in alignment with the job/company)*

➔ **O** = Outcomes – Value you have added. *(In alignment with and relevant to the job/company)*

End = *An Ask: Ask to stay connected, request a meeting, ask for the interview (as appropriate)*

➔ Engage in the conversation authentically. Maintain curiosity. Ask questions, focus on the company, the job, and the person.

➔ Obtain the person's contact information, ask for a business card, and/or request connection via LinkedIn. Request a follow-up meeting or an interview (as appropriate).

➔ Gracefully and professionally end the conversation.

YOUR PITCH OUTLINE

Use the space below to create your conversational pitch outline.

Introduction:

_____

_____

Middle:

_____

_____

_____

_____

_____

_____

_____

_____

_____

_____

_____

_____

_____

_____

_____

End:

_____

_____

_____

_____

MARKET READINESS — LINKEDIN HEADLINE & SUMMARY

RECALL MOMENT – VALUE MATTERS!
Way back in Chapter 1, I asked the following question: *Why does almost every aspect of the career journey require evidence of value?*

The answer: because **value matters.**

Almost all decisions we make include an assessment of value. The products we buy, the experiences we engage in, the work we do, the companies we love, the jobs we apply for, the raise we request, the promotion we seek. It's all connected to value.

Knowing your value is good for you. Valuation builds confidence and helps you build your brand. When you know your value, you can confidently leverage your value to negotiate for a raise, promotion, or new job.

Your declaration of value happens by deploying WHO Logic.

Another important market readiness tool is LinkedIn, a premier professional networking platform. Networking prior to LinkedIn was challenging. LinkedIn is diverse in offerings and includes the ability to search and apply for jobs, among other options for professional growth and advancement.

Your LinkedIn profile is a marketing tool that advertises your value and is segmented into areas that correspond with market readiness tools including value proposition, resume, and the conversational pitch.

For example, the segment in your LinkedIn profile referred to as the *headline* is a perfect spot for a simplified version of your value proposition.

LINKEDIN HEADLINE

Take a look at my LinkedIn headline: *Career Design Strategist | WHO Logic Evangelist*

LinkedIn defaults the headline to your most recent job title, so if I didn't use the edit function to change my headline, you would see my job title, *Associate Director.*

What unique attributes and value does the title "associate director" convey? Not much comes to my mind, how about you?

So, I use the headline as an opportunity to share my unique attributes and the core of WHO I am. My headline is derived from my value proposition. The two are very similar. My LinkedIn headline and my value proposition are declarative descriptions of who I am.

HOW TO WRITE YOUR LINKEDIN HEADLINE

Prepare your value proposition using WHO, then simplify it for your headline. It's that easy! Less than 10 words is optimal, as you are using the headline to hook your reader.

LINKEDIN ABOUT SECTION

Your LinkedIn profile includes an *about section,* a perfect spot for your entire value proposition, highlights from your career, and a declaration of where you are headed. Here's my LinkedIn summary:

I am a career design strategist who uses empathy, creativity, and WHO Logic to help people become market ready and advance professionally.

My professional passion is deeply rooted in supporting the goals of students, alumni, and colleagues. Contributions within the university setting include strategic planning, assessment, and outcome-driven career education. Design thinking and deep learning experiences are my latest curiosities.

You can see that I lead off my LinkedIn about section with my value proposition. I then share my primary passion; I mention my career focus areas and conclude with my latest curiosities.

ANCHORING YOUR VALUE PROPOSITION IN YOUR HEADLINE AND THE ABOUT SECTION OFFERS SEVERAL ADVANTAGES

The first advantage has to do with repetition. Repetition is useful to learners. Anyone who reviews your LinkedIn profile is a learner. They are reviewing and absorbing information about you. You want enough repetition in your profile to help them recall. Please remember how learning happens. Your reader is introduced to information—your headline mentions attributes and perhaps a working title. These attributes are repeated in your about section and throughout the resume portion of your profile. The learning becomes sticky. **You are remembered.**

The second advantage is for you. By repeating your value proposition throughout your LinkedIn profile, you affirm your core, who you are, the attributes and skills you can leverage, your outcomes. Your value proposition, your WHO, becomes you.

I am a career design strategist who uses empathy, creativity, and WHO Logic to help people become market ready and advance professionally.

WHO Are You?

TURNING IT ON – YOUR JOB-SEEKING ASSISTANT

Once the headline and about sections have been added, you need to complete the remaining segments of your profile. ***Turn on your job-seeking status*** by updating your account settings and privacy section to ensure recruiters easily find you. If you need additional help using LinkedIn, I recommend LinkedIn's own content, www.university.linkedin.com/linkedin-for-students.

CHAPTER END & NEXT UP

Building from the resume, value proposition, and cover letter development, we used Chapter 6 to continue the valuation journey by exploring conversational pitch and LinkedIn profile development. These market readiness tools represent the self-marketing required for lifelong career management.

Next up, we're putting your market readiness tools to work and going to market. The job market, that is...

See you there!

7

Launching into the Job Market
Matchmaking Your WHOs with Their WHOs

Hello, WHO Logic learners! Welcome to Chapter 7. By this point in the book you have created a WHO-infused resume and value proposition. You are well-versed using WHO to help you form an aligned, value-centered cover letter. You have explored the conversational pitch with Jane T. Avatar, and you can use these market readiness tools and tips to build your LinkedIn profile. Great work!

Much like a company launching a product into the consumer market, you launch into the market when you share your seeking status as active and when you apply for jobs.

Throughout the previous chapters we applied *What, How,* and *Outcome* to develop your market readiness tools. As a result, you know WHO you are, meaning you have evaluated your experiences to generate evidence of value. We also used Jane T. Avatar to practice **alignment** with jobs and companies as part of the market readiness process, particularly with the cover letter and conversational pitch.

Why do you need to align? (*I am confident you know, but I am offering a gentle reminder.*) Because a seller (you) must pay attention to the interests and needs of buyers (employers) in order to produce a sale. The seller adjusts the *product* pitch accordingly. This doesn't mean the product is fundamentally altered to attract a buyer. It means the statements of value shift and align based on buyer interests and needs.

HAVE YOU GUESSED WHERE WE ARE HEADED IN CHAPTER 7?

More alignment! Using the principles of how we learn, we're diving a little deeper into the very important partnership between WHO Logic and alignment during the job search and networking process. We're applying WHO Logic as a **matchmaking** tool. Yep, it's all about the love.

MARKET READINESS TOOLS ADJUSTMENT & ALIGNMENT

Your market readiness tools adjust and align for several reasons.

1. The tools adjust based on alignment with jobs and companies of interest.
2. Your tools adjust as a result of your professional growth and progress.

Keep your market readiness tools ready! This means the ongoing use of WHO Logic to inventory and assess your experiences.

JANE T. AVATAR AND MATCHMAKING

JANE T. AVATAR AND ALIGNMENT WITH UVW CORPORATION

Jane T. Avatar's alignment with the marketing internship at UVW focused on customer engagement via digital marketing. She used specific value points from her resume and cover letter to align with the job posting and company. She even pulled language directly from the job posting in her cover letter and pitch to target the alignment.

Jane is actively engaged in the job market. Up to this point in the book we have focused on Jane's interest in UVW Corporation. She is actually applying for many internships, and she aligns based on what she understands about the job and company. Jane *aligns her WHOs with job and company WHOs.*

JANE T. AVATAR AND ALIGNMENT WITH THE QSR INDUSTRY

If Jane T. Avatar is applying for a marketing internship at corporate headquarters within the quick service restaurants (QSR) industry, also known as the fast food industry, she will align accordingly. Let's say that one of the preferred qualifications is experience in fast food. This is perfect for Jane. She can highlight the value she added while working in QSR at Taco Bell. She's aligning and connecting.

JOB APPLICATIONS & MATCHMAKING

Actively seeking and applying for jobs means you have launched into the market. Applying for jobs requires *preparation and ongoing adjustment of market readiness tools, submitting applications, and networking.* At this point in the job search process, you are foundationally market ready. You will need to make slight adjustments to your tools, but the foundation has been built. Your resume, cover letter, value proposition, and pitch are evidence-based, value-centered, and ready for action.

APPLYING FOR JOBS
PREPARING AND SUBMITTING JOB APPLICATIONS – FINDING JOBS

You can find job postings using a variety of online tools. The most prominent job posting system today is Indeed. LinkedIn and Glassdoor have also become dominant players, and if you are currently a student enrolled in college, your career services center will likely use a job posting system such as Handshake.

There are many job posting sites. Some are very niched, based on industry or functional area, so you may have to conduct a little research. You are resourceful. I trust you will identify the best job posting system(s) for you.

PREPARING AND SUBMITTING JOB APPLICATIONS – FOLLOW INSTRUCTIONS

This may seem obvious, but please follow all instructions for applying to the job. Some job posting systems allow you to apply directly within the system, and some redirect you to the company website. Some companies contract the entire hiring process out to a third party. Regardless, follow the job application instructions.

PREPARING AND SUBMITTING JOB APPLICATIONS – ATS SYSTEMS

Let's return to applicant tracking software systems for a moment. Please recall that ATS systems are used by many companies (buyers). When you apply for jobs in the *public job market*, you are competing with hundreds, perhaps thousands of applicants (sellers). ATS systems help identify the most relevant (aligned) applicants based on parameters set up by the company.

You must align. That's all there is to it. ATS systems are programmed to pick up relevant keywords from the job posting. The keywords typically relate to skills and qualifications (Your *How* in WHO).

> **RECALL MOMENT!**
> **What Are Market Readiness Tools?**
> Anything that provides an opportunity for you to promote your value, including but not limited to the following:
>
> → Resumes, Cover & Thank You Letters
> → Value Proposition & Pitch
> → LinkedIn Profile
> → Networking & Interviewing

> **PUBLIC JOB MARKET**
> The term *public job market* means that you are applying to jobs that everyone has access to via the internet by way of job posting systems like Indeed, LinkedIn, and Glassdoor.
>
> The challenge is that you are competing in a relatively small buyer's market and a very large seller's market. Your market readiness tools must be centered in value and align with the job and company of interest.

PREPARING AND SUBMITTING JOB APPLICATIONS – MATCHMAKING STEPS

Let's recall the matchmaking process using WHO Logic. Your goal is to identify and assess the job and company WHOs, then align with your WHOs. That's a lot of assessment and alignment, but it's worth your time. Please recall that it is really your job to identify value, alignment, and fit, then sell it.

PRACTICE MATCHMAKING — STEPS FOR ALIGNING YOUR WHOS WITH THE JOB & COMPANY WHOS

Step 1: Apply WHO Logic to analyze the job description to determine alignment.

→ **WHAT** does the job do? *(circle or highlight the job tasks, duties, responsibilities)*

→ **HOW** does the job get done? *(circle or highlight skills, qualifications needed)*

→ **OUTCOMES** produced by the job? *(identify and articulate the value the job adds to the company; also consider the outcomes associated with your professional growth)*

Step 2: Find the alignment. Follow the prompts below:

→ Do your WHOs and the job WHOs align?

→ Match your experiences—align your skills and value with the job tasks, duties, and responsibilities.

→ Do your value points align with the value this role adds to the company and is there potential for professional growth?

Step 3: Apply WHO Logic to analyze the company culture and proposition of value.

→ **WHAT** does the company do? *(mission, core focus, what is produced)*

→ **HOW** do they do the work? *(values, unique attributes, innovations, strategies)*

→ **OUTCOMES?** *(value-add, deliverables, impact)*

◀ Note that the **What** and **Outcomes** could be similar in step 1 and step 3.

Step 4: Find the alignment. Follow the prompts below:

→ Do your WHOs and the company WHOs align?

→ Match your experiences and interests in alignment with the company culture and proposition of value.

→ Do you share similar values with the company? Review their "About Us" web page.

→ Align your value points with the company, and consider the potential for your professional growth.

⚙ WHO INVENTORY & ALIGNMENT EXERCISE (MATCHMAKING)

Try this! Google a job title of interest. Your search will likely deliver many relevant job postings. Select one job posting of interest and research the company.

Step 1: Inventory: Move horizontally in the table and inventory the job posting and company using WHO Logic to help you respond to the questions.

Step 2: Alignment: Review your resume. List relevant experiences, skills, and outcomes that align with the job WHOs and company WHOs.

INVENTORY		
What does the company do? **What** does the job do? *(responsibilities, tasks, duties)*	**How** does the company do the work? *(values, innovations, unique differentiators)* **How** does the job get done? *(required skills, qualifications)*	**Outcomes** produced by the company and job?
ALIGNMENT		
Experiences Alignment - What *Your Relevant Tasks, Projects*	***Skills Alignment - How*** *Your Relevant Skills/Experiences*	***Outcomes Alignment*** *Your Relevant Value*

➜ What did you find? Did you align with the job and company?

CHAPTER END & NEXT UP

You made the match! Go ahead, hit the "Submit Application" button. Okay, you have WHOified the job and the company. You aligned their WHOs and your WHOs. At minimum, you will send a resume, and hopefully you will take the time to prepare a cover letter, as this is helpful for your preparation.

Your resume is in great shape with your most relevant value statements prominently displayed. Your value proposition is clear. Your cover letter is spot-on in terms of alignment with the job and company. And you could pitch at a moment's notice. You hit the submit button to send your application materials.

Whew, done! Nope! There's more. You need Fast Networking. Read on...

8

Networking

Fast Networking and Slow & Steady Networking

In Chapter 7 you put your market readiness tools to work and launched into the job market by way of applying for jobs. The logical next step in the job search process might be to focus on interview preparation. Rest assured, the positioning of networking within the book is quite purposeful. Market readiness and career advancement rely heavily on two forms of networking, *fast networking* and *slow and steady networking*.

Fast networking is singular in purpose and focused completely on gaining advocacy from someone who works at a company with an open position. This situation happens when you identify a job of interest, typically from a posting in the public job market. Either shortly before submitting application materials, or immediately after, you reach out to one or more people working at the company to seek quick advocacy.

Slow and steady networking is exploratory and starts with list making. The emphasis is not on a specific job, but on companies and people of interest. Yes, you likely want to work at the company, but you either are not ready or there isn't a current job posting. This is not fast networking. Slow and steady networking centers around learning and building reciprocal and value-centered relationships, particularly with people who are working at companies of interest.

Do you know the adage, "getting a job is all about who you know"? It's true. Google something like *"what percentage of getting a job is connected to networking?"* You might be surprised. Regardless of the various percentages quoted, the message is clear. Networking matters. Let the networking begin!

FAST NETWORKING & WHO LOGIC

Just when you thought hitting the submit button to send your application materials was enough, along comes fast networking. You really can be the best candidate for a job, but when you apply through the public job market, there is a chance your application could be overlooked. I know, super disappointing, especially since you spend significant time with valuation and alignment. How is it possible to be overlooked when you are the best? (fig. 7)

Please allow me to share this unfortunate scenario. Let's use Jane T. Avatar to illustrate. Jane is a great candidate for a marketing internship at the corporate headquarters of a well-known and very profitable fast food company. Let's go so far as to say that on paper she is the best candidate out of 500 applicants for this coveted role.

Jane applies for the job and the ATS system helps narrow the number of good-fit candidates to 150 applicants. Jane makes it through the initial cut and is part of the 150.

Of the 150, 10 applicants have either long-standing or fast-networked relationships with employees at the company. Because of the internal advocacy and referrals, these 10 rise to the top of the resume pile and it is this group of 10 applicants who will likely advance to the status of interviewee.

fig. 7 ▼

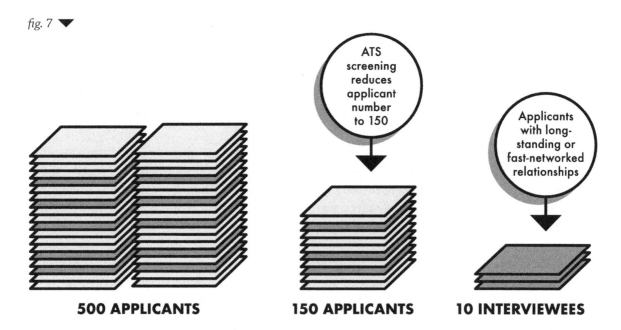

500 APPLICANTS   **150 APPLICANTS**   **10 INTERVIEWEES**

Don't get me wrong, they all made it because they are strong candidates. Jane didn't, not because she isn't a strong candidate. Remember, she's the best. It's just that she doesn't have an advocate at the company. This scenario demonstrates how competitive the conversion from applicant to interviewee can be.

INTERNAL COMPANY REFERRALS/ADVOCACY – UNFAIR OR NOT?

Many students I have worked with over the years tell me they think referrals or advocacy to the top of the resume pile is unfair. The thinking is, the person just got the job because they know someone at the company.

A long time ago, before I started working in career services in the university environment, I thought so as well. I don't anymore. I believe the smartest thing a person can do is network. In fact, everyone should set aside at least one to 10 hours each week to build and engage their network. One hour if you are not job-seeking but are maintaining and slowly growing an established network. Ten or more hours each week if you are actively job-seeking. More about this as we move into slow and steady networking.

FAST NETWORKING MECHANICS

Here's how fast networking works. When you apply for jobs in the public job market, (LinkedIn, Indeed, Glassdoor, Handshake, or other job posting sites), and you don't know anyone at the company, you should include *fast networking*.

Either just before or immediately after you apply for the job, identify *several* people at the company and send a customized connection request via LinkedIn or send an email. Here is a suggested hierarchical order for finding people at the company using LinkedIn:

➜ Alumni from university/universities attended

➜ Someone working in the functional area of interest who isn't necessarily a fellow alumnus/alumna

➜ Some other affiliation or affinity (from the LinkedIn profile—similar volunteer interests, hobbies, other affiliations or affinities)

➜ Anyone from the company that stands out for you (it could be they just have a nice smile)

Any form of ***advocacy*** from someone working at the company has the potential to add strength to your application. Reach out to several individuals from the company, particularly those working in the business unit or functional area of interest. I'm including a few message samples to show how you can customize your LinkedIn connection request. You can also send the message by email if you have an address. You can even try calling if you have a phone number.

Fast Networking Message Suggestion, Alumni:

"Hello, fellow [insert school mascot]! I'm hoping I can request some help. I just applied for a position with [Company Name]. I'm wondering if you might be willing to talk this week. Your insights and advice would be much appreciated. Thanks for considering this request. Sincerely, [insert your name]."

Fast Networking Message Suggestion, Non-Alumni:

> *"Greetings! [brief description of who you are—e.g., I'm a student at Great State University] and I just applied for [position name] at your company. I'm wondering if you might be willing to talk this week. Your insights and advice would be much appreciated. Thank you for considering this request. Sincerely, [insert your name]."*

You may have to adjust your note depending on affiliation and length, due to character limitations in LinkedIn's connection request messaging function.

Here's the thing about fast networking: (1) It's fast. (2) You have nothing to lose and everything to gain. If your message is professional and polite, you are not offending anyone. In fact, you are demonstrating initiative, confidence, assertiveness, and a sincere interest in the company.

If after three business days a connection is not made via LinkedIn, try someone else at the company. If you are reaching out via email and have not received a response after five business days, send the message again. I have found that a second attempt can yield connection. You can also try by phone using the company phone number. Again, if you are professional and polite, your persistence can pay off. If after two attempts you don't receive a reply, I typically advise moving on.

For a larger company, you may wish to reach out to more people. More volume in your outreach has a greater chance of yielding a connection. At a small or medium-size company, targeting one or two people is usually enough.

WHAT HAPPENS AFTER THE CONNECTION IS ACCEPTED?

You tried fast networking and you made connection with a person who agreed to chat with you for 15 minutes by phone. Awesome! The call is scheduled. Now what? The cool thing is, you are so ready! Remember your market readiness work? You know your WHOs, the job WHOs, and the company WHOs. You have assessed and aligned. Your resume is strong, your cover letter aligns. You know your value proposition. ***You are ready to pitch!***

SO, IT'S A PITCH? YES, FAST NETWORKING IS A PITCH WITH A SLIGHT ADDITION

Prior to the conversation, you should engage in a ***person-centered WHO inquiry exercise***. Take a few minutes to explore the person's experience and background. Your ability to do this is heavily reliant on the information available. Don't sweat this if you can't find much. You might have to extrapolate and infer. Focus on the person's What and Outcome(s) to support your conversation.

Person-Centered WHO Logic*

→ **W = WHAT** does this person do? *(job title, responsibilities)*

→ **H = HOW** do they do the work? *(skills, strategies, innovations)*

→ **O = OUTCOME(S)** produced? *(value-add, impact, deliverables)*

◀ *Information can be extrapolated from LinkedIn profile, company website, Google search.*

THE FAST NETWORKING CONVERSATION, LIKE THE PITCH, REQUIRES IMPROVISATION

The fast networking conversation is outlined as follows:

Fast Networking Conversation: The Introduction – *Includes what you want*

Introduce yourself, thank this person for their time, and inform them that you have just applied or are about to apply for a job (include job title and any other pertinent details). Let this person know you are hoping to gain some insights about the job and the company based on their experience, and that you welcome any advice that could help strengthen your chances for employment with the company. Because you are asking for advice from this person, it's possible you may chat for quite some time about their experience. That's okay and this is why you should conduct a person-centered WHO inquiry prior to the conversation.

Fast Networking Conversation: The Middle – *Use WHO to provide evidence of value & alignment*

At some point in the conversation, you need to provide a quick 60-second overview of your resume *and* a 60-second highlight of how you align with the job and company.

Fast Networking Conversation: The End & The Ask

Pay attention to time. This conversation shouldn't take any more time than what you requested, usually 15–20 minutes. When you are getting close to 15–20 minutes, be sure you have provided an overview of your background and have shared aligned value points from your resume. You then need to ask for an endorsement. Ask this person if they might be willing to put in a good word for you with the hiring manager and/or HR. You may also ask if there is anyone else at the company this person might recommend you speak with to support your application.

Remember your primary goal. You need advocacy, someone to endorse your value and alignment with the job.

If you need help to prepare for the fast networking conversation, review the section on pitch. Fast networking is essentially a pitch. It's other-oriented, with a focus on providing evidence of your alignment with the job and company and your potential to add value.

Your fast networking conversation may also include a fair amount of time learning specifically about this person and their experience working at the company. That's great! The more information you obtain, the better understanding you develop about the job and company in relation to your interest and fit for the role.

Be curious and use empathy to engage this person. They are giving you time, and this is an opportunity for you to learn. During the conversation, **be aware** of this person's level of engagement. If the person is helpful, shares information and advice, and perhaps even extends the call beyond 15 minutes, it's possible this relationship has the potential to develop into a long-lasting professional relationship.

You have invested time to produce evidence of value and alignment, and the job market is competitive. Believe me, you want your value to be known. Utilize every advantage you can create for yourself. Because you used WHO Logic to assess and align, you will have plenty to ask and share during your fast networking conversation.

By the way, referrals and endorsements that come from employees within the company are very helpful in the application process. Some companies even reward employees for referring job applicants.

Fast networking is aptly named. It is a quick outreach strategy to gain advocacy for a specific job opportunity. Most individuals express trepidation when I introduce fast networking. They are afraid this outreach will be perceived as disingenuous or cheating. I quickly work to help them reframe this thinking. You are not cheating by reaching out to someone for help. If you are polite, professional, and sincere in your interest in the job and company, your efforts will be well received. People participate in LinkedIn for this very reason.

FAST NETWORKING WITH YOUR EXISTING CONTACTS

You may have met a recruiter or someone from the company at a recruiting event or some other engagement. Just because you have interacted with someone once or twice in advance of submitting your application doesn't mean they are standing by waiting to advocate for you. You need to reach out when you submit your application materials so they are ready to advocate for you.

To further illustrate, let's return to Jane T. Avatar. Recall her conversational pitch to Zunerah Martin from UVW Corporation. They had a pleasant exchange and it's likely Jane left a positive impression. The final and unwritten step for Jane in the application process is to inform Zunerah that she submitted application materials, and she needs to thank her for sharing information and support, along with asking for advocacy.

In this situation, Jane might send an email including the following:

"Hello, Zunerah. Thank you for a great conversation during the UVW networking event on February 9 at GSU. I learned a great deal from our chat and wanted to let you know, I just applied for the marketing internship. I'm including my resume for your reference and would very much appreciate any form of advocacy you can offer to support my application. Thanks so much for considering this request, and I look forward to your reply. Sincerely, Jane T. Avatar."

TARGET YOUR FAST NETWORKING

I suggest your fast networking be targeted more toward people who are working in the functional area or business unit relevant to the job you are seeking. I call them *practitioners*. Beyond the possibility of gaining quick advocacy from your fast networking efforts, networking with a practitioner typically means you learn more about the actual job from a primary source.

Students often ask me if they should fast network with HR professionals, particularly recruiters, whose role is dedicated to talent engagement and acquisition. You can; just know their influence in the hiring decision varies.

The exception to my advice about targeting practitioners rather than HR professionals is, of course, if you aim to work as an HR professional.

TRY FAST NETWORKING

Please let me remind you that LinkedIn is specifically designed to serve as a professional networking platform. Anyone who has a presence on LinkedIn is essentially saying they are available to interact. If you are still hesitant about fast networking, ask yourself what would *you* do if someone from your school, your hometown, or some other affiliation reached out to you via LinkedIn and politely shared their interest in you and your job, and requested to connect and briefly speak with you?

If that's not enough encouragement, then consider this: fast networking can improve your chance for advocacy and is better than just hitting the job application submit button and hoping a machine or a human takes notice.

The primary goal for fast networking is very targeted—to obtain advocacy, quickly. Fast networking does offer the opportunity to build a long-lasting relationship, but the primary intention is to obtain an endorsement to support your job application.

SLOW & STEADY NETWORKING & WHO LOGIC

Unlike fast networking, you aren't starting with a job application; you start with the idea that the company and person are of interest to you. Your networking focus is on learning and building reciprocal and value-centered relationships, particularly with people who are working at companies of interest. Be patient. Slow and steady networking requires sincere interest, curiosity, and a communication plan.

Your relationships build from a place of authenticity and alignment. You represent WHO you are honestly and professionally, and connection happens when you establish shared interest and value with the other person.

Before we explore the mechanics, allow me to introduce you to the origins of slow and steady networking. My background includes working at several universities with little to no *employer pipeline*, meaning that employers don't line up to recruit students. Please know that a small or nonexistent employer pipeline has no reflection on the quality of the school. There are many reasons associated with this circumstance, including majors not aligned with local industry needs, too much competition from nearby universities, and specialized recruiting with a very tiny footprint on the entire campus. I could provide many other reasons, including extreme economic downturns, but very few have to do with the quality of education.

I share this background with you because much like the WHO valuation framework for resumes, slow and steady networking developed as a response to need. When employers don't flock to campus, the solution is to teach strategies that help job seekers take the lead in connecting with companies and people.

The other reason for teaching people how to build a networking strategy has to do with the fact that on-campus recruiting is a rare instance in a person's life. This idea that a bunch of employers (buyers) and job seekers (sellers) come together in a crafted environment to buy and sell isn't the norm. It's an unusual moment. In the market readiness class I teach, I help prepare students for the oddity that is "fall recruiting," and once the frenzy is nearly over, I set a scenario in class whereby an *on-campus recruiting apocalypse* occurs, resulting in the complete demise of on-campus recruiting. Students must then build a networking strategy. The goal with this exercise is to reinforce the idea that networking is a critically important practice to get a job, to professionally grow, and to advance one's career.

The original networking guide and communication tracking spreadsheet I created was designed to help computer science majors with the job search after the dot com crash. I no longer have the original documents from the early 2000s, but I can see the sample outreach tracking spreadsheet in my mind's eye. It was very simple and looked a little bit like this:

NETWORKING TRACKER – **SAMPLE**

Company Name	Company Highlights	Contact Person	Contact Type	Initial Outreach	Outreach Results	Outreach	Results	Outreach	Results
0101 Incorporated	20% market share, progressive, new CEO	Chester Boone, director and alumnus	Advocate	Emailed on 1/16; Called on 1/26	Helpful, provided advice on courses and strategies to help my job application	Sent article about company from Technical Times periodical on 3/2	*Continue to keep track*	*Continue to engage*	*Continue to keep track*

Although this spreadsheet is quite simple, it's the foundation for slow and steady networking. The idea was to help students keep track of relationship building and gain advocacy to help land a job.

The spreadsheet from the early 2000s evolved into a **Networking Guide**, a **Networking Funnel**, and a **Communication Tracker.** The guide and funnel can be found in the following pages. The communication tracker can be found in the appendix.

THE SLOW & STEADY GUIDE AND THE FUNNEL

Let's review the guide and the funnel. The guide is designed to provide an outline for your networking **practice**. I use the term *practice* to represent a regular action, a normal part of your life routine.

The guide (pages 90–91) offers multiple steps to support your networking and relationship development practice. Step 1 focuses on the development of market readiness tools and Step 2 offers suggestions on how to generate a list of companies and jobs of interest. Step 3 highlights the use of LinkedIn to identify people who work in jobs and at companies from your list. The remaining steps emphasize outreach and relationship development by engaging people who have potential to become supporters and advocates.

The funnel (page 92) illustrates the scope and scale of converting prospects to advocates (fig. 8). The top of the funnel represents prospects, individuals who are working in jobs and at companies from your list. It is through your outreach and engagement that conversion happens, the narrowing from prospects to contacts, contacts to supporters and advocates.

NETWORKING & RELATIONSHIP DEVELOPMENT GUIDE

"Getting a job is all about who you (get to) know"

1. NETWORKING PREPARATION –
GET STARTED WITH COMMUNICATION TOOLS:

→ Build your resume and LinkedIn profile—join groups
→ Develop your value proposition and pitch
→ Generate relevant outreach messages

2. MAKE A LIST OF COMPANIES, JOBS & PEOPLE OF INTEREST

COMPANIES & JOBS

→ Job posting sites: Handshake, Indeed, LinkedIn, Glassdoor, and Internships.com
→ Google: *"best companies for [functional area(s) of interest]"*
→ Google: *"best mid-size/small companies to work for [industry - location]"*

PEOPLE (PROSPECTS)

→ Professional associations and publications; referrals from faculty, staff, friends and family
→ Identify people (prospects) working at companies and jobs of interest using LinkedIn
→ Start with a list of 30–40 people (prospects)
  • You may need hundreds of prospects (fig. 8)
→ Prepare for LinkedIn request to connect
  • Be ready to share *why* you are interested in the person/company/job

3. COMMUNICATION & OUTREACH –
CONVERT YOUR PROSPECTS TO CONTACTS:

→ Reach out to prospects and request connection via LinkedIn
  • Personalize the message
→ Once connected, the **prospect** becomes a **contact**; ask for an informational interview

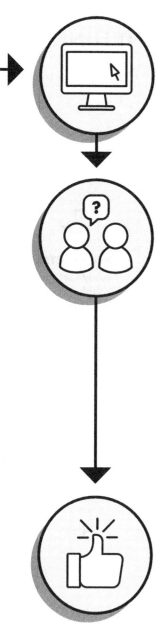

4. **PREPARE FOR THE INFORMATIONAL INTERVIEW –
   USE A CURIOUS MINDSET TO GUIDE YOUR RESEARCH:**

   → Prepare by conducting research on your contact, the job, the company, the industry
   → Make note of interesting highlights, innovations, and accomplishments; generate "curiosity" questions

5. **THE INFORMATIONAL INTERVIEW –
   ASK CURIOSITY QUESTIONS; DISCOVER WHAT MATTERS
   TO YOUR CONTACT:**

   → Take notes; use the information from the conversation to help you learn about your contact, the industry, the company and job
   → Use the results of your research to ask "curiosity" questions about the industry, company, job of interest, and your contact
   → Ask about meaningful and value-add priorities and projects your contact has completed within the past six months
   → Ask about projects and priorities your contact would like to pursue
   → Ask for advice about investments you can make to support your professional development
   → Follow up with a thank you note and value/validate the time your contact has given

6. **CONVERTING CONTACTS TO SUPPORTERS/ADVOCATES**

   → Build a communication plan, develop touch points for outreach to engage your contacts
   → Share information with your contacts—related to their projects and priorities and your mutual interests
   → Let your contacts know you followed the advice offered; stay in contact—perhaps every 8–12 weeks
   → Record your communication activity using Excel or some other project management app

NETWORKING & RELATIONSHIP MANAGEMENT FUNNEL

Conversion of Prospects to Advocates

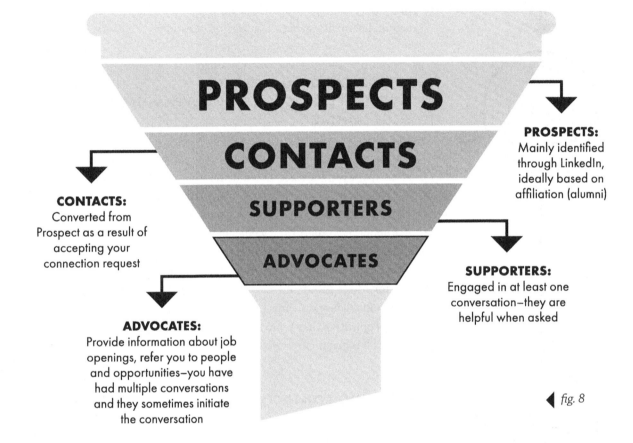

PROSPECTS

CONTACTS

SUPPORTERS

ADVOCATES

PROSPECTS:
Mainly identified through LinkedIn, ideally based on affiliation (alumni)

CONTACTS:
Converted from Prospect as a result of accepting your connection request

SUPPORTERS:
Engaged in at least one conversation—they are helpful when asked

ADVOCATES:
Provide information about job openings, refer you to people and opportunities—you have had multiple conversations and they sometimes initiate the conversation

◀ *fig. 8*

Build relationships by launching and maintaining an effective, authentic, and sincere communication plan with the goal of converting **prospects** to **advocates** whenever possible.

SLOW & STEADY NETWORKING – USING WHO TO GET TO WHY

Once you build a list of companies, jobs, and people of interest, your initial research helps answer why you are interested. **Why** is incredibly important! Without the **why**, your initial outreach will fall flat. You must be able to share with people why you are reaching out, why you are interested. If you don't share the why, you run the risk of being ignored. The cool thing is, **WHO helps answer why!** Just wait, you'll see.

If you deploy WHO Logic as an inquiry framework, you can use the results to guide your **outreach and communication.**

Here's what WHO Logic looks like for company and person inquiry and valuation:

Company Assessment *(Discovering the company WHOs)**

→   **W** = What does the company do? *(mission, what is produced)*

→   **H** = How do they do the work? *(company values; unique attributes, strategies, techniques)*

→   **O** = Outcome(s) generated by the company? *(value-add, deliverables, impact)*

▲
Information can be sourced from company website, LinkedIn, Glassdoor, press releases, Google search, company research databases (typically through library systems)

ASK YOURSELF:
→   Do you love what the company does?
→   Do you value what the company values?
→   Is the company's value-add exciting to you?

Person Assessment *(Discovering the WHOs for the person of interest)**   ◀ *Information can be extrapolated from LinkedIn profile, company website, Google search.*

→   **W** = What does this person do? *(job title, responsibilities)*

→   **H** = How do they do the work? *(skills, strategies, innovations)*

→   **O** = Outcome(s) produced? *(value-add, impact, deliverables)*

ASK YOURSELF:
  → Do you love what this person does?
  → If you can tell how this person does the work, is that appealing to you?
  → Is the person's value-add exciting to you?

Self-Assessment

  → **W** = What do I do and what have I done relevant to the company/person?

  → **H** = How did I do the work? *(skills, strategies, and tools that are relevant to the company)*

  → **O** = Outcome(s) associated with my experiences? *(value-add, contributions, learning)*

NOW WHAT? ALIGNMENT – EXCITEMENT – INSPIRATION
  → Do you find alignment between your WHOs, the company WHOs, and the person WHOs?
  → Can you now or in the future add value to the company?
  → Are you excited by what you have discovered about the company and the person?
  → Are you inspired to professionally grow in alignment with the company goals?

Answering these questions helps you answer **why** you are interested.

AN ILLUSTRATION OF SLOW & STEADY NETWORKING BROUGHT TO YOU BY JANE T. AVATAR

Jane's networking strategy includes a list of 15 companies of interest from the QSR industry. (Recall moment: QSR = quick service restaurants.) She identifies one company of interest, MNO Energy. A LinkedIn search identifies four alumni currently working in marketing functions at MNO Energy corporate headquarters. Here you will find an example of Jane's effort to prepare for connection with one of the four alumni.

THE RESULTS OF JANE'S COMPANY RESEARCH USING WHO – MNO ENERGY

What do they do?

Mission: Generate fast, nutritious food to fuel busy individuals and families. Number 8 in QSR revenue generation nationwide. Staffs the largest nutrition unit in the QSR industry.

How do they do the work?

By being mission-driven, with a heavy reliance on employee input, which drives strategy. By leading digital marketing innovation within the QSR industry. Using a nutrition focus and sustainable business practices. By offering unique and limited menu items with inexpensive and high-quality ingredients. Company values: people first, quality, connection.

Outcome(s) Intended/Produced?

To be Number 5 within 5 years. To grow market share. To focus on fast nutrition. Ranked within top 100 companies to work for from a work/life balance perspective. Considered a "thought leader" in the QSR industry.

THE RESULTS OF JANE'S PERSON RESEARCH USING WHO – MARJORIE DOE @ MNO

What does she do?

Director on the Consumer Perception Team. She focuses on changing consumer perception of fast food restaurants.

How does she do the work?

Uses the company mission as her anchor. By leading the nutrition outreach campaign for the company, by partnering with digital marketing and nutrition business units, and by obtaining celebrity endorsements.

Outcome(s) Intended/Produced?

To change perception of fast food. To solidify the niche – fast nutrition. To increase revenue and market share.

JANE T. AVATAR FINISHES THE WHO VALUATION

This takes about 20 minutes with a quick review on LinkedIn and within the "About Us" page on the company website, as well as a look at Marjorie Doe's LinkedIn page. Jane spends a few minutes aligning to help her prepare the LinkedIn connection request.

Jane starts with her value proposition: *Emerging marketing professional who builds relationships and boosts profit by leveraging collaboration, initiative, communication, and technical skills.*

She aligns based on her skills and experiences including her digital marketing work. Like Marjorie, Jane has spent time collaborating and building relationships to meet customer engagement and revenue generation goals.

Jane can reach out via LinkedIn, or she can send an email if she locates Marjorie Doe's email address.

Jane T. Avatar's Connection Request Message on LinkedIn

> *"Greetings, fellow Great Stater! I am an emerging marketing professional pursuing a BA at GSU. Your background in fast nutrition, collaboration, and technology is inspiring. Please accept my request to connect. Thank you! Jane T. Avatar."*

EMAIL CONNECTION TIP:

People are busy. If they don't respond to your connection request within 5 business days, it's likely not a rejection.

Send your request a second time. Wait 10 business days. If nothing, try a third time and if you don't receive a response within 10 days of your third attempt, let it go for a while.

Try again in about two or three months if you haven't already connected with someone else at the company.

www.linkedin.com/in/jtavatar"

Jane T. Avatar's Request to Meet via Email

> *"Greetings, fellow Great Stater! I am an emerging marketing professional pursuing a BA at GSU. Your background in fast nutrition, collaboration, and technology aligns with where I am trying to go. I have worked in the QSR industry and am focused on developing a career in marketing. I am wondering if you might have 20 minutes within the next two weeks to chat with me about your experience. Advice from you would be most appreciated. Thank you for considering this request.*
>
> *Sincerely,*
>
> *Jane T. Avatar*

JANE ANSWERS THE QUESTION WHY?

Because Jane used WHO Logic to value and align, she answers the question **Why**. There is a higher likelihood the individual will accept if you express why you are requesting connection. Jane highlights fast nutrition, collaboration, and technology, extracted from Marjorie's LinkedIn profile.

You may be asking yourself, all that inquiry work to value and align for one short message on LinkedIn or via email? Yes, and I'm confident you will thank me for nagging you about valuation and alignment.

INFORMATIONAL INTERVIEW

Once the person accepts your connection request, it's time to ask for a brief meeting, an *informational interview*. Remember, you are trying to build relationships and perhaps even develop an advocate.

Let's assume Marjorie accepts the request to connect via LinkedIn. Jane T. Avatar will follow up by sending a thank you and requesting an informational interview.

> The informational interview is an opportunity for you to talk with someone working in a job and/or at a company of interest.
>
> Your goal is to learn about the person and the company. You are gathering information by interviewing your person of interest.

Jane will work to find a convenient time for Marjorie to meet with her, likely by phone, unless the two are in the same city, then an in-person meeting may be possible.

Here comes WHO Logic again. The effort Jane put into the valuation and alignment will be used to prepare for the informational interview.

Jane has created a WHO Logic profile for MNO Energy. She knows what the company does, their mission, values, and actual and intended outcomes. Jane also created a WHO Logic profile for Marjorie. She uses results from WHO inquiry and valuation to formulate **curiosity questions** in preparation for the informational interview.

Curiosity questions come from a place of authentic interest and are often influenced by the results from WHO inquiry and valuation.

POSSIBLE CURIOSITY QUESTIONS JANE MIGHT ASK DURING THE INFORMATIONAL INTERVIEW WITH MARJORIE *(drawn from research and WHO valuation)*

Jane selects several questions from her list and the conversation is rich with information to help Jane better understand Marjorie's role, the business unit, and the company. Here is Jane's question set:

- I'm very impressed with MNO Energy's mission. How do you use the mission to guide your work?

- I know the company is striving to be Number 5 in the nation within 5 years. How will your unit influence this progress?

- Can you share with me a bit more about how you partner with the digital marketing unit?

- Your work engaging celebrities and using their endorsements to change the perception of fast food is really interesting. Can you share with me the impact of these efforts?

- What specific projects have you worked on that have been most influential/impactful for the company?

- What projects would you work on if you had more time?

- What advice do you have for me as an emerging marketing professional?

USING VALUE POINTS TO ALIGN AND SHARE DURING THE INFORMATIONAL INTERVIEW

Just like the pitch, Jane will need to find her conversational moment to align and share her value. Jane can expound on many statements of value from her resume.

Let's duck in on a portion of the informational interview between Jane and Marjorie.
Look for Jane's use of relevant **value points**:

Jane:
> "MNO Energy is using very innovative digital marketing strategies to change the perception of fast food. I have had some experience using digital outreach to engage and persuade. I currently work as a University Guide at GSU. This is an outreach position, and one of my projects includes email and social media outreach. I send over 50 email and social media outreach messages per month to build relationships and persuade prospective students to attend GSU. There is so much competition and usually students have admission offers from multiple schools, so it's been a great learning experience to help influence prospects to convert to applicants."

◀ **Use your resume!** An expansion of a relevant **value point** from Jane's resume, in alignment with Marjorie's role at MNO Energy.

Marjorie:
> "Yes, we are most certainly challenged by competition as well. Our unique value proposition lies in fast nutrition. GSU has a unique value proposition as well. I remember when I was a student, it was all about being a graduate who could roll up her sleeves and work really hard. You certainly seem to be embracing that value."

And the informational interview continues to conclusion. Jane will send Marjorie a thank you message within 24 hours after the conversation. Jane asked many of the questions she prepared based on her WHO-influenced preparation and she took careful notes during the informational interview. She will utilize this valuable information from Marjorie by using periodic communication touch points to further develop the relationship over time.

When an internship or full-time job becomes available at MNO Energy, it's possible Marjorie will reach out to Jane directly and urge her to apply, with Marjorie's full endorsement. It's also possible Jane might need to ask Marjorie for an endorsement. Either way, if she has converted Marjorie from a contact to a supporter or advocate, Jane will likely get the endorsement.

Additionally, it's important to remember that Jane will continue to grow professionally, regardless of whether she works for MNO Energy. If she maintains contact with Marjorie and a deeper relationship forms (with as little as one or two interactions each year) both parties experience value in the relationship.

WHEN THE "CONTACT" STATUS DOESN'T CONVERT TO SUPPORTER OR ADVOCATE

Jane reaches out to a ***Prospect*** she identified on LinkedIn, Mark from GHI Company. Mark accepts the connection request and an informational interview occurs.

Additional communication efforts by Jane do not result in converting Mark to a *supporter* or an *advocate*. There could be many reasons why he is less responsive than Marjorie at MNO Energy. This doesn't mean Mark will remain in the status of "contact" forever, but Jane's consistent effort indicates her time may be better spent cultivating other relationships.

> **LIE FALLOW**
> A Farming **and** Networking Term.
> When a farmer lets a parcel of land go uncultivated, it's said the land lies fallow. Like the land, sometimes your contacts need to lie fallow as well.

Based on her needs and interests, Jane decides to let Mark lie fallow for a few months as she prioritizes other relationships. You may notice this in your outreach and communication as well. As the shape of the networking funnel indicates, it's normal to have many contacts that don't convert to supporters or advocates. Despite the effort required to identify prospects and the work required to convert, it takes just one supporter or advocate to make a difference in your job search or career advancement. I suggest you do the work. It's critically important.

A ROBUST NETWORKING PRACTICE REQUIRES KEEPING TRACK OF THE EFFORT

Jane will organize and record her relationship-building activities using a communication tracker. You can use a project management app or a spreadsheet to guide and record your networking engagement. ***Please take a look at Jane's communication tracking mechanism in the appendix.***

SLOW & STEADY NETWORKING TIPS & REMINDERS

BUSY PROFESSIONALS WANT TO KNOW THEIR TIME IS VALUED AND VALUABLE

When someone gives you advice, referrals, or any other information that supports your career growth, value their time. For example, if your supporter advises you to explore joining a relevant professional organization, explore the organization and let your supporter know how valuable this advice is to you. Let the person know what you learned as a result of the exploration. Value their time. They want to know the time they gave you was useful. This tip holds true for fast networking as well.

PERSISTENCE, NOT STALKING

Need I say more? Yeah, probably.

Prospects to Contacts: You might reach out to a prospect, perhaps on LinkedIn. You patiently wait. Days pass. When is the time right to send another message? I typically advise 5–7 business days and then send your message again (second attempt). Wait another 5 business days and consider trying a different form of communication, such as using a work email address or phone number if you can locate this information. People are busy and it's my belief that most want to be helpful. If you attempt to connect two or three times within a 6-week period with no results, you can move on and perhaps return to this prospect later.

Contacts to Supporters/Advocates: Once your contact has agreed to chat with you and if this conversation goes well, you must use care to build out this potential relationship. Do not reach out too often. Slow and steady. For example, during a 6-month period, you may wish to reach out two to three times. Make sure your content is interesting and relevant to your contact. For example, if you know your contact is interested in the reduction of jobs due to technological advances and you come across an article produced by a reputable source, send it.

DON'T ASSUME YOU ARE BOTHERING PEOPLE

You are not in their head. You don't know. If they are not interested in chatting with you, let them tell you that. Be professional, polite, and persistent. If the person is unresponsive after several attempts, move on and let this situation lie fallow. You can always come back much later.

KEEP TRACK – STAY ACCOUNTABLE TO YOUR NETWORKING GOALS

You could easily be working all aspects of the funnel at any given time; prospect development, outreach to contacts, or researching something related to one of your supporters. This means you have a lot going on. Use some form of tracking tool. The communication tracker noted in the appendix represents a very simple sample. Many free project management apps can be found online and can help guide and record your efforts.

NETWORKING = FRIENDSHIPS

Your primary goal with slow and steady networking is to build valuable relationships that are mutually beneficial. Networking is about making professional friendships. If a job opportunity results, great! If not, the relationship can be meaningful in many other ways. Your supporter and advocate connections grow and change as you professionally progress.

CURIOSITY + A GROWTH MINDSET + COURAGE + PERSISTENCE = GRIT

Grit is incredibly important. This might be the most important part of networking. You need grit. There will be moments during your networking activities when you feel defeated. People are unresponsive, you can't seem to convert prospects to contacts. People are unavailable for informational interviews or the interaction doesn't seem to yield much. It's okay. Your efforts will produce supporters and advocates. Just keep going. Grit.

NETWORKING PRESCRIPTION – JOB SEEKER

In my advising practice, I often use a prescriptive approach. The student provides an overview of their job search and networking activity; together we review and customize a next-step strategy. The thing about networking is that you don't get paid to do it (it's typically not part of your job) and it isn't an assignment to complete for a grade.

Here's a sample "networking prescription" developed with a job seeker who wanted to network during a holiday break and expressed the need for help in two areas: (1) to expand the job search beyond Fortune 100 companies, and (2) outreach to undeveloped contacts.

NETWORKING PRESCRIPTION

Prospect Generation

➔ **Identify 3–4 target geographies** - Google *"Best companies to work for – small/medium size."* You can also omit size as a parameter and just see what returns you get with *"best companies to work for [location]."*

➔ **Identify 10 companies** of interest for each geographic target. Apply WHO – *What* does the company do? *How* do they do the work? (mission/values/culture), *Outcomes* (value produced, deliverables). Use *Glassdoor* for a quick review. The company should be on your list if you feel an alignment with your WHOs.

➔ **Check LinkedIn** for alumni affiliations. Also check functional areas. You can always cold call people working in your functional area of interest who are not alumni.

Prospect to Contact Conversion

➔ *Outreach message suggestions using LinkedIn*

Alumni Affiliation:

> *"Greetings fellow [insert mascot name]! I discovered you by researching outstanding companies in [location]. I am eager to learn more about [company name] and would appreciate the opportunity to chat with you. Please consider this request to connect. Sincerely, [Your Name]"*

Non-Alumni:

> *"Greetings! I discovered you by researching outstanding companies in [location]. I am eager to learn more about [company name] and would appreciate the opportunity to chat with you. Please consider this request to connect. Sincerely, [Your Name]"*

Contact to Supporter/Advocate Conversion

For individuals who respond to your outreach by accepting connection, ask for an informational interview. From this point, work toward building the relationship and converting contacts to supporters and advocates.

Reach out to your existing contacts. Given the time of year, send a seasonal themed message, particularly to individuals you have met within the past year. You may even want to create a prioritized list. You could send something like the following message:

> *"Season's Greetings! I hope the holiday period is filled with warmth and happiness. I recall our conversation(s) this past fall and appreciate the advice you offered. Thank you again. It would be great to catch up with you sometime soon, perhaps early in January. For now, please enjoy the season. Warm regards, [Your Name]"*

→ **Curiosity, Empathy, and Joy.** Find the attitudes you need to help guide your networking and job search journey. Then live the attitudes. Let's see what you can generate from this outreach. Please keep track using a spreadsheet or project management app. I'll see you in 3 weeks.

As you can see from the prescription networking requires a lot of self-discipline. You need to build a strategy and you need to dedicate time. I often indicate to a job seeker that I will serve as an accountability partner and we set up regular meetings, just to touch base. I'm not a nag, but I have learned that if individuals I'm working with have to follow up with me, they tend to do the work. Find an accountability partner, use a prescriptive approach, and make networking a regular practice.

THE VALUE OF SLOW & STEADY NETWORKING FOR CAREER EXPLORATION

Just like slow and steady networking for job seekers, a **_career explorer_** can use slow and steady networking to help discover career options.

MAKE YOUR LIST OF COMPANIES, JOBS & PEOPLE

A career explorer starts by making a list of companies and jobs of interest, then conducts research and reaches out to people at the companies and/or in the job roles, mainly using LinkedIn. Like trying on clothes, the goal with career exploration is to "try on" jobs. And this can be done by communicating with people who are working in jobs of interest.

USE WHO LOGIC AS AN INQUIRY AND VALUATION FRAMEWORK

Follow the networking guide highlighted earlier in the chapter. Just like Slow and Steady Networking for Job Seekers, use WHO Logic as an inquiry and valuation framework, helping you determine **_why_** you are interested in the company, job, and person. The sample communication messages included here can be very effective to initiate conversation.

OUTREACH – MESSAGE SUGGESTIONS USING LINKEDIN

Alumni Affiliation:

"Greetings fellow [insert mascot name]! I am working on a BA/BS and discovered you by researching outstanding companies in [location/industry type]. I am eager to learn more about your experience and would appreciate the opportunity to chat. Please consider this request to connect. Sincerely, [Your Name]."

Non-Alumni:

"Greetings! I am working on a BA/BS at [University Name] and discovered you by researching outstanding companies in [location]. I am eager to learn more about you and would appreciate the opportunity to chat. Please consider this request to connect. Sincerely, [Your Name]."

> **RECALL MOMENT!**
> **Mindset** – If you need help with risk taking and trying stuff, read Carol Dweck's Mindset. Build your growth mindset. It's good for career exploration!
>
> **Designing Your Life** – If you need prototyping inspiration, read Designing Your Life by Bill Burnett & Dave Evans. You will find practical tools to help you try stuff.

Follow the outreach and communication steps in the Networking Guide. Approach the networking process with curiosity!

WHAT COMPANIES, WHAT JOBS, WHAT PEOPLE? HOW TO GET STARTED WITHOUT A LIST

Starting with a list of companies and jobs can be daunting for a career explorer, especially if you have no idea what companies or what jobs. If you prefer to gather a bit more information about yourself before you embark on a networking journey, you can start career exploration by taking a survey to help you better understand your values, interests, and skills. This knowledge may help you identify occupational areas of interest which can then help with your company, jobs, and people list. There are several surveys available via the internet and many that yield results connected to jobs, including "16 Personalities," available at www.16personalities.com.

Here's another issue to consider. If you are a young person reading this book, know that your career will likely change dramatically during your lifetime. Due to technological advancements and the pace of change, jobs that exist today will not look the same in the near future, and many will be gone. Your future likely includes *upskilling*, which essentially means lifelong investment in learning new skills.

I share this new world order of continuous learning to emphasize that it's fine if you are uncertain about your career because it will likely change multiple times—and that's okay.

You need curiosity to explore your interests and you need empathy to align your *authentic interests* with employers' interests.

NETWORKING PRESCRIPTION – CAREER EXPLORER

Here's my ***prescriptive approach*** once again, this time developed with an undergraduate student who needed help getting started with career exploration. This student happened to be interested in working with animals or art to help people overcome mental health challenges.

Generating the List of Jobs & Companies

Develop a list of 5–15 different job titles of interest.
Once complete, select your top 5 job titles. Use Indeed.com to build your list.

Using www.indeed.com:

- → Enter keywords like *Criminal Justice, Social Services, Animal Care, Animals, Art, Art Therapy, Juvenile Justice, Youth Advocacy, etc.*
- → After you enter keywords, select *"Find Jobs,"* then select *"Entry Level"* to generate a list of jobs representing an appropriate experience level.

Deploy WHO Logic – Inquiry & Alignment

From the top 5 **job titles**, select 5–10 **job postings** of interest.
Review the job postings and run a quick WHO Logic inquiry to build a job WHO profile.

- → **WHAT** does the job do? *(responsibilities, duties)*
- → **HOW** is the job accomplished? *(skills, qualifications)*
- → What are the **OUTCOMES** for the job? *(what value does the job produce)*

Review the company associated with the job. Run a quick WHO Logic inquiry to build a company WHO profile.

- → **WHAT** does the company do? *(mission, what is produced)*
- → **HOW** do they do the work? *(company values, unique attributes, strategies, techniques)*
- → **OUTCOME(S)** generated by the company? *(value-add, deliverables, impact)*

Assess & Align Your WHOs with the Company and Job WHOs

Ask yourself:

- → Are you interested in what this job does?
- → Do the skills and qualifications connect with you?
- → Do you love what the company does?
- → Do you value what the company values?
- → Is the company's impact exciting to you?

Remember, you are only using Indeed as a mechanism to explore. Be open to exploring any job title that looks interesting to you. Your next steps include identifying people at the company who are doing work interesting to you and then using the networking guide to help you build an outreach and communication plan.

☼ YOUR TURN! BUILD YOUR LIST OF COMPANIES, JOBS & PEOPLE

Job seeker or career explorer, you can get started by making a list of companies based on the resources provided, along with your own creative ideas. Use LinkedIn to identify people of interest working at the companies on your list. Use WHO Logic as an inquiry and valuation framework and start reaching out.

CHAPTER END & NEXT UP

From a job search perspective, your goal with *fast networking* is to find quick advocacy, to increase your ability to rise to the top of the interview list by way of a supportive referral from someone who has an affiliation with the company of interest.

Your goal with *slow and steady networking* is to convert prospects into supporters and advocates. The goal is similar to fast networking, but the process is slower. Slow and steady networking does not yield a job within days or weeks. This is a long-term relationship-building experience that unfolds and evolves based on authentic and reciprocal value-centered exchange. Not all contacts will convert to supporters and advocates.

From a *career exploration* perspective, your goal with slow and steady networking is to learn and narrow your interests to help you build an initial career path. Recall that your career will change throughout your lifetime. The important note here is to select a starting point.

Networking is a very important part of the career exploration and career advancement process. You can work hard and value your experiences, but you don't grow and progress in isolation. Develop reciprocal value-centered relationships when the vibe feels strong, when the person, job, and company align with your goals and interests, and when the professional pheromones are positive.

Use curiosity, empathy, and a growth mindset to help you explore and build relationships. Let networking be a lifelong practice and you will be pleasantly surprised at your career advancement.

Next up, we journey into the world of interviewing using WHO Logic as a preparation tool and as a robust response framework for interview questions. We'll join Jane T. Avatar as she interviews for the marketing internship with UVW Corporation.

Let's see what happens...

9

Interview Preparation

Welcome to Chapter 9, *Interviewing!* Our ***valuation mindset*** journey continues. Now that your evidence-based resume includes persuasive value points, and your cover letter, value proposition, pitch, application strategies, and networking activities are value-centered, and you are able to align your skills and experiences with jobs and companies, you are ready for interviewing.

In this chapter, we will use WHO Logic as a preparation tool for interviews ***and*** as a response framework for most of the questions you will encounter during the interview. Before we explore the use of WHO for interviewing, let's consider the purpose of an interview.

INTERVIEW PURPOSE

Much like networking, your goal with an interview is to provide three things:

1. ***proof of your ability to add value***
2. ***evidence that you align with the job and the company***
3. ***authentic enthusiasm for the job and company (fit)***

This is why the introductory question *"Tell me about yourself"* is so important. It sets the tone for the interview and offers you the opportunity early in the conversation to share value, offer evidence of alignment, and represent your authentic enthusiasm. We'll take a closer look at this introductory question later in the chapter.

Here's the other thing you can't forget about the purpose of an interview. It's an opportunity for you to assess fit for *your* professional wants and needs. You learn about the company via the people you speak with during the interview. You experience the culture of the organization through the interaction you have with the interviewer(s). You ask curiosity questions that help you become more knowledgeable about the opportunity. This is your chance to learn about how the job and company can add value to your professional growth.

What I'm saying here is that the interview is a ***two-way, reciprocal assessment of value, alignment, and fit.*** You certainly need to prepare, and you need to help the interviewer(s) understand how you align with the job, while you are also exploring value, alignment, and fit for yourself.

As much as an interview might conjure feelings of interrogation, a bright light burning into your forehead, an inhospitable interviewer and other associated unpleasantries, it's really not. The interview is a *conversation*, designed to help all participants figure out value, alignment, and fit. A conversation means improvisation. Please recall the segment on pitch. **Be yourself.** Be prepared but don't be a bot. Need help relaxing into an interview (and life)? Read *Improv Wisdom* by Patricia Ryan Madson.

REFLECTION MOMENT

Before moving on, please answer the following questions.

- ➜ **WHAT** is the purpose of an interview?
- ➜ **WHAT** do you want the interview to be like for you?
- ➜ **HOW** do you want to represent yourself during the interview?
- ➜ **HOW** do you want the interviewer to represent the job and company?
- ➜ What **OUTCOMES** do you anticipate from authentically representing your value and alignment?

INTERVIEW PREPARATION USING WHO

This segment of the chapter involves the use of WHO for interview preparation, to help you focus on value and alignment. Why? Because value and alignment matter in hiring decisions. If you need help with interview basics such as what to wear, what to have with you during an interview, nonverbal communication tips, panel interviewing, web-based interviewing, or other associated preparation topics, check with a career advisor or use tools from reliable online resources.

Our work with interview preparation brings us back to **WHO Logic Inquiry, Valuation, and Alignment**. Every market readiness tool you have created for this one amazing job you want culminates with the interview. Figure 9 represents how we arrived at this point:

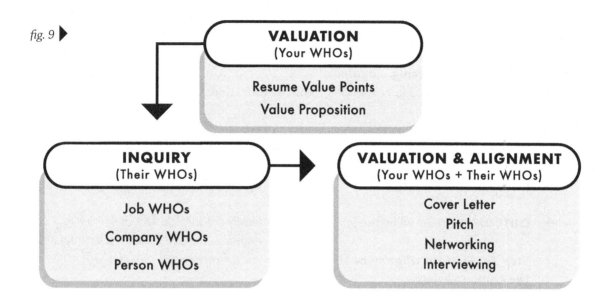

fig. 9 ▶

VALUATION
(Your WHOs)

Resume Value Points

Value Proposition

INQUIRY
(Their WHOs)

Job WHOs

Company WHOs

Person WHOs

VALUATION & ALIGNMENT
(Your WHOs + Their WHOs)

Cover Letter
Pitch
Networking
Interviewing

In preparation for the interview you have developed:

→ A WHO-engineered resume with evidence-based value points
→ A value proposition that reflects WHO you are at your professional core
→ A strong understanding of the job and company based on WHO inquiry and alignment
→ A WHO value-centered and specifically aligned cover letter
→ The ability to pitch your value in alignment with the job and company

You should also strategically use your network. Ask your contacts, supporters, and advocates from the company to share advice and tips in advance of the interview. This is a key step and yet another demonstration of the importance of relationship building through fast and slow and steady networking.

REPETITION, RECALL, AND ELEVATED PRACTICE BRINGS YOU TO THE INTERVIEW

This entire market readiness process is filled with repetition, recall, and elevated practice, one activity after another using WHO Logic to prepare you for the job market, culminating in the interview.

Think about it: by the time you receive an invitation to interview, the company has screened your marketing tools (i.e., resume, cover letter, LinkedIn account, etc.), so during the interview, your work is really about reinforcing your value and alignment and demonstrating your authentic enthusiasm and professionalism.

INTERVIEW PREPARATION EXERCISE

Your preparation is a refresher, based on the work you have already produced. Let's return to aligning your WHOs with the job and company WHOs. **Before your interview, move through this exercise.**

Step 1: Review the job posting… again.
Apply WHO Logic to identify job tasks **(W)**, skills/qualifications **(H)** and value **(O)**.

◀ *Note that the **What** and **Outcome** could be similar.*

→ **WHAT** does the job do?

◀ *Circle or highlight the job tasks, duties, responsibilities*

→ **HOW** does the job get done?

◀ *Circle or highlight the skills and qualifications needed*

→ **OUTCOMES** produced by the job?

◀ *Identify and articulate the value the job adds to the company; also consider the outcomes associated with your professional growth*

Step 1a: Find the alignment. Follow the prompts below:
- Match your experiences—align your skills with the job qualifications, tasks, and responsibilities
- Align your value points (from the resume) with the job qualifications, tasks, and responsibilities

Step 2: Apply WHO Logic to analyze the company culture and proposition of value.

→ **WHAT** does the company do? *(mission, core focus, what is produced)*

→ **HOW** do they do the work? *(values, unique attributes, innovations, strategies)*

→ **OUTCOMES**? *(value-add, deliverables, impact)*

◀ *Note that the **What** and **Outcome** could be similar.*

Step 2a: Find the fit and alignment. Follow the prompts below:
- Match your experiences and interests with the company culture and proposition of value
- Match your values with the company values (Review their "About Us" page)
- Align your value points with the value the company adds

Step 3: Return to your resume and cover letter, identify each value point in alignment with the skills and qualifications of the job. You may even want to complete the cover letter matchmaking alignment exercise from Chapter 6.

THE VALUATION & ALIGNMENT RELATIONSHIP

fig. 10 ▶

GENERAL INTERVIEW QUESTION STRUCTURE

Interviews can take many forms. I use a basic question category structure when helping students prepare for interviews. We'll review each category and use Jane T. Avatar's interview for the UVW internship as an opportunity to look at responses.

Interviews typically include the following question categories:

→ Introductory Question
→ Behavioral Questions
→ Scenario/Situational Questions
→ Common Questions
→ Technical Questions
→ Your Questions for the Interviewer

INTRODUCTORY QUESTION

I believe the introductory question is magical! Your response to this question sets the stage and helps the listener understand your value, alignment, and energy. You really do have the opportunity to pull your listener in and get them excited about what's to come.

The introductory question provides the perfect moment for you to hook the listener. *"Tell me about yourself"* is most often positioned at the beginning of the interview and can be asked in many ways: "Tell me about your background," "Walk me through your resume," "Share your academic and professional history." Regardless of the specific language, the question is really asking, *"Tell me about yourself, and how do you align with this job and the company?"*

This question offers you an opportunity to confidently share relevant parts of your background in alignment with the job and company. Your response is an expansion of your value proposition and similar to a conversational pitch. It's a summary of WHO you are, what you have to offer, and how you can deliver value.

I advise job seekers to provide a response to the intro question that is about 90 seconds in length and not more than two minutes. The first few seconds might start with the value proposition, then move to a high-level overview of the resume, and the second portion of the response is dedicated to articulating value and alignment.

JANE T. AVATAR – INTERVIEW FOR UVW MARKETING INTERNSHIP POSITION

Let's follow along with Jane T. Avatar *during* her interview with the hiring manager in the Customer Experience unit at UVW, a leading staffing and training firm.

Jane's Response to the Introductory Question:

Interviewer: *"Jane, thanks for taking time to meet with me today. I have reviewed your resume and have a good understanding of who you are on paper. Can you take a few minutes to tell me about yourself?"*

Jane: *"Thanks for offering this opportunity to chat! I'm excited to share my background and learn more about the internship. I am working on a Bachelor of Arts in marketing and will finish in a year and a half. I see myself as an emerging marketing professional with skills using digital tools to enhance the customer experience. I am a creative person who takes initiative, and I'm eager to work as part of a team focused on boosting profits using innovative marketing practices.*

I offer relevant experience including the development of a digital marketing campaign that yielded increased sales, while I was working at a locally owned restaurant. I have worked in a quick service restaurant where I was ranked first in district sales, and I'm currently working as a University Guide for the school, where I use persuasive communication to influence enrollment; and my digital marketing skills include the use of InDesign, Tableau, and Google Analytics.

I am really excited about UVW. When I read the company values on your website, I felt very aligned. I have demonstrated entrepreneurialism in each job I have held, and every job has been focused on customer satisfaction and use of technology, attributes that UVW describe as important and valued. I am confident I have the skills you are looking for and I believe the internship offers a great opportunity for professional growth."

➔ **Has Jane hooked the listener with aligned and value-centered statements?**

BEHAVIORAL QUESTIONS

Behavioral interview questions are incredibly common and are used to help an interviewer predict how you would behave on the job with them. ***The questions are often connected to skills, qualifications, and responsibilities taken directly from the job description.*** Your responses help the interviewer understand previous behavior and predict future behavior.

It's also important to note that the best way for an interviewer to determine how you will add value to their company is to understand how you have added value in the past.

WHO is an excellent framework to develop examples you can offer as evidence to help your listener value and align your experiences with the job and the company.

You can almost always tell when the behavioral question is coming your way because the question typically starts with "Tell me about a time when...," or "Can you give an example..."

The WHO Logic framework to help you construct a response for behavioral (and most) interview questions:

WHO Framework:

➜ **W** = What was the situation or context?

➜ **H = HOW** did you manage the situation? *(skills, strategies, methods used)*

➜ **O** = Outcome(s) produced from the work? *(value-add, impact, results, your learning)*

Behavioral-based interview questions lean on the ***How*** portion of the framework. Certainly, outcomes matter in behavioral interview questions and you should always close the loop by providing an outcome, but it is the *how* in a candidate's response that many employers emphasize.

Again, we return to prediction. Understanding how someone managed a previous situation helps an employer better predict future behavior while learning more about relevant skills and qualifications of the candidate.

Jane's Response to a Behavioral Question:

Interviewer: *"Can you tell me about a time you used persuasion to influence an outcome?"*

Jane: *"Sure. While working for a small local restaurant as a delivery driver, I regularly heard from customers how much they loved the food, and many asked me about coupons and specials. I also noticed the social media presence was nonexistent and I thought it would be a good idea for the restaurant to advertise using social media. After sharing customer feedback and my technical skills and ideas about incentives, I persuaded the owner to let me build a social media campaign using Facebook and Twitter. With my boss's involvement, I built a communication plan offering coupons and incentives and utilized Google Analytics to measure traffic. Within six months of launch the restaurant experienced a 25% increase in revenues. This was a valuable experience for me and has influenced my future career path. I am happy to say that the restaurant now has a social media person on contract, and their sales continue to be better than before the use of social media!"*

WHO Spotting & Response Analysis:

→ Can you spot the use of WHO Logic in Jane's response?
→ Can you identify how using WHO helps provide proof of value and alignment?

TECHNICAL QUESTIONS

Technical questions relate to knowledge or skills specific to the job. Don't be misled by the term; *technical questions* aren't necessarily associated with technology (software or hardware abilities). Technical questions relate to skills and experiences needed for working in a specific job or industry. For example, an interview for a helping professions position might include a technical question about active listening techniques or best therapeutic practices to help individuals overcome a crisis. Given that Jane T. Avatar is interviewing for a marketing internship with UVW Corporation, the following technical question is appropriate for the role.

Jane's Response to a Technical Question:

Interviewer: *"You mention using Google Analytics to generate data for marketing and sales. Can you tell me a bit more about this experience?"*

Jane: *"Yes, while working at the Village Pub, I built our social media presence and used Google Analytics to help us understand if our marketing campaigns influenced sales. Specifically, I used the campaign tracking feature to help us determine the impact social media campaigns had on delivery orders versus in-house dining. By using the tracker, we understood that orders for delivery were 50% higher than orders for in-house dining. The ability to order and use discount coupons from our newly developed social media accounts produced more sales for our delivery service. The campaign tracker from Google Analytics helped us know exactly where the increase in sales volume was coming from and how we might use the data in the future."*

WHO Spotting & Response Analysis:

→ Can you spot the use of WHO Logic in Jane's response?
→ Can you identify how using WHO helps provide proof of value and alignment?

SITUATIONAL QUESTIONS

Situational questions pose a *"what would you do"* scenario and, like most other interview questions, help predict how you will behave and perform on the job. I categorize situational questions into two types.

SITUATIONAL QUESTION, TYPE 1:

The first type of situational question is often quite basic and asks about general skills and situations associated with the job. Very early career professionals (first jobs, early college internships) will likely receive this basic type of situational question.

The interviewer may overtly say they have a situational or scenario question and they want you to walk them through what you would do. They may also just say, "tell me what you would do if…," or "tell me how you would handle…"

Jane's initial response answers the question without an example from her experience. WHO Logic is present as she provides *what* she would do, *how* she would do the work, and an intended *outcome*. Beyond the initial response, because she can, Jane will strengthen her answer by offering a relevant example.

Jane's Response to Situational Question, Type 1:

Interviewer: *"Can you tell me what you would do if you were asked to lead your peers in a team project?"*

Jane: *"Yes, of course. I would take on the role using a servant leader approach. I would make sure my team had what they needed to get each task accomplished and I would take responsibility for keeping us organized, for managing our communication, and for making sure we meet our deadlines."*

(Because she can, Jane will strengthen her response by providing an example. You should always aim to include an example.)

Jane: *"I experienced something similar in a course I had last semester. Our instructor placed the class in groups of six students to complete a research project in 12 weeks, with a paper and presentation as our final product. Our first meeting included an agreement that someone in our group should lead the team. I volunteered and shared that I would take on the responsibility for organizing the tasks and helping us put together our action plan. My team agreed and I kept us focused and on task. I created a Google document, shared among all of us, and I took the lead to keep the document current with assignments, targets, and deadlines. When team members were struggling, they came to me for support and I helped them find the resources they needed to complete the work. I also helped break down the tasks into smaller chunks to make it easier for us to achieve our goals on a steady basis, so we weren't overwhelmed with large tasks and short deadlines. I communicated with the team three times each week with updates, offered to help if anyone fell behind, and celebrated our successes using fun text messages and emails to keep us connected and engaged. We completed the paper in advance of the final deadline, and our presentation was voted number one by the class for best data and graphics."*

WHO Spotting & Response Analysis:

→ Can you spot the use of WHO Logic in Jane's response?
→ Can you identify how using WHO helps provide proof of value and alignment?

SITUATIONAL QUESTION, TYPE 2:

The second type of situational question is often used with a more experienced professional. The question typically asks about a specific problem or challenge that may require use of your technical skills.

This type of situational question is similar to a question style used in the consulting industry referred to as "case interviewing." Case interview questions are typically complex and test a variety of skills including analytical and technical skills. Situational questions are typically not as time-consuming or complex as case interview questions. However, both are used to predict how you will behave and perform on the job.

Please know that Jane's response to the question may include many moments of exchange between the interviewer and Jane. It depends on how involved this situational question becomes. Be ready for a situational question to take anywhere from 3 to 20 minutes. Use WHO Logic to help you frame the response.

WHO Logic Framework for Type 2 Situational Questions:

→ **W** = What is the situation or context?
   (You will likely need more information beyond the question asked of you. This means you should not just launch in with a response. You should ask some clarifying questions to ensure you understand the situation.)

→ **H = HOW** will you manage the situation?
   (What strategies, methods, techniques, skills will you deploy to do the work)

→ **O** = Intended Outcome(s) produced from doing the work?
   (The intended value-add, impact, and contribution)

Jane's Response to Situational Question, Type 2:

Interviewer: *"Jane, what would you do if you were given a new customer segment to explore for our company?"*

Jane opens her portfolio and confirms with the interviewer that it's okay to take some notes as she is preparing to work on this situation.

Jane: *"I have a few questions, just to get some clarification on the situation. Is it okay with you if I sketch out some of my thoughts while we talk?"*

Interviewer: *"Of course. Yes, what are your questions?"*

Jane: *"So, this is a new customer segment for the company. Can you share with me the current landscape of this segment? Are they using the service our company offers, but with a competitor? Can you provide a bit more demographic information as well as any insight on consumer preferences and behaviors about this prospective customer segment?"*

Interviewer: *"This segment isn't currently using the service. Much of this has to do with the fact that our company's core focus is staffing, more often used by millennial and baby boomer generations. Currently, the service is offered at our site offices around the country. The targeted customer segment is an age range between 17 and 25. They are referred to as iGens and have essentially used technology their entire lives. They are most often in college or college-bound. Their parents are generally middle class, have likely been to college, and are eager to ensure the career success of their children."*

Jane is taking notes. She pauses and asks one more question before moving forward.

Jane: *"What is the service?"*

Interviewer: *"It is a service that offers training to help this customer segment become job-market ready and advance in their career using a nimble valuation tool to evaluate, articulate, and leverage their value."*

Jane: *"Okay, let me think about this for a minute or two."*

Jane sketches out the situation using WHO. She leaves plenty of room on the page for the *How* section.

- ➜ **WHAT** is the situation? A job-market readiness service being offered to an age range of 17 to 25 years, middle class, iGens.
- ➜ **HOW** – Focus on the marketing mix (4 Ps).
- ➜ Intended **OUTCOME** – Build and retain the customer segment – Establish targets, year 1, year 2, etc.

Jane's Situational Interview Sketch

<u>WHAT is the situation?</u>

A job-market readiness service being offered to an age range of 17–25 years, middle class, iGens. Company is well-known and successful staffing firm.

Here's what I recall from class on basic demographics: approximately 328 M people in the U.S.; about 20 M in college—about 65 M iGens. iGens are "streamers"—approximately 71% have Netflix subscriptions, they hate ads, and 65% of them think salary is important. They are likely going to be interested in something that helps them leverage their value.

<u>HOW (possible strategies)</u> – My ideas for how we explore expansion into this segment:

4 Ps – Product, Price, Place, Promotion

Product: Review the competition—what are they offering and how; Product positioning—ensure this service is distinct from competition. Need to modify and make this service accessible online to grow the market; accessible via smartphones.

Price: What is the value of the service to this customer segment? What is the typical price point for something similar? Are we in the range? Pricing flexibility. Strength of core competency may make it possible to enter market with high quality/lower price.

Place: On-site and online, with the emphasis online. This is where they are!

Promotion: Emphasis is here. No to outbound marketing—they don't like it and don't respond. Use a content and engagement marketing approach.

1. Use content marketing (pull)—build videos, podcasts, blogs, social media.

2. Start a campus ambassador program—train college students to be mini subject matter experts—relationship development focus with cost-effective boots on the ground.

3. Search engine optimization (SEO).

<u>INTENDED OUTCOMES</u> – Build the customer segment—establish sales targets and benchmarks for years 1, 2 & 3. Use analytics to gain insights about segment and use data to inform decisions.

Jane's Response to a Situational Question:

Jane: "Let me share my thoughts on how I would explore this potential customer segment. I would first use basic demographics about this population to inform me of their general attributes and behaviors. Here's what I recall from a class on basic demographics: there are approximately 328 M people in the U.S.; about 20 M in college—about 65 M iGens. iGens are "streamers"—approximately 71% have Netflix subscriptions, they hate ads, and 65% of them think salary is important. They are likely going to be interested in something that helps them leverage their value.

I'm using the 4Ps to support my ideas for how we explore expansion into this segment with an emphasis on **promotion**.

Product: I will review the competition to understand what they are offering and how. We'll need to look at product position to ensure our service is distinct from the competition's and that we are positioned in a way that speaks to and meets this segment's unique needs. To do so, I would suggest modifying and making the service accessible online to grow the streamers market. I would also explore making the service accessible via smartphones.

Price: I will want to understand the value of the service to this customer segment. I think it's valuable given that this population generally considers salary to be important, and this could be the type of service that resonates with iGens. I'll need to know the typical price point for something similar and look at our current pricing ideas. I would suggest pricing flexibility given that this is a new product, and we may be able to afford a loss for a while given the strength of the core business of UVW. We might be able to enter the market with high quality at a lower price.

Place: Given the investment in on-site learning locations, we should continue to use them and measure the usage in numbers. We absolutely need to offer the service online and via mobile, as this is where they are!

Promotion: Emphasis is here. I suggest very little outbound marketing—they don't like it and don't respond. I am suggesting an emphasis on content and engagement marketing.

1. Use content marketing (pull)—build videos, podcasts, blogs, social media.

2. Start a campus ambassador program—train college students to be mini subject matter experts—relationship development focus with cost-effective boots on the ground.

3. Explore the use of search engine optimization, maybe Google Adwords. Although a bit more outbound, I think we could see some results through SEO.

The intended outcome is to build and retain the customer segment. We want them coming back once they've tried the service, to build strong customer lifetime value.

Measurement is key. We will need to establish sales targets and benchmarks for years 1, 2, and 3. We need to use analytics to gain insights about this segment and use data to inform decisions. We'll use what we learn from the data and sales numbers to determine if the segment is worth growing and pursuing beyond year 3."

WHO Spotting & Response Analysis:

→ Can you spot the use of WHO Logic in Jane's response?
→ Can you identify how using WHO helps provide proof of value and alignment?

UNKNOWN TYPE OF QUESTION

Sometimes you will be asked a question that doesn't seem to fit into a category. Is it behavioral? Is it a common question? What is it? Sometimes it's hard to tell. That's okay, just reframe the question. The goal is to provide an example. Use WHO Logic as your framework and you will be fine. Check out what Jane does with the following question.

Jane's Response to an Unknown Type of Question:

Interviewer: *"How do you feel about working in teams?"*

Jane: *"I enjoy collaboration and working in teams. It's an opportunity to learn from others and to share my knowledge. Great teamwork can produce great results. Let me give you an example of how working in a team can be incredibly beneficial. In my current role as a University Guide, I was asked by the marketing director to generate content for a social media campaign aimed at high school freshmen. I was really struggling with content ideas and reached out to my University Guide peers. Among this group, we realized that six of us had siblings in this age range. We put them on a group chat and they helped us develop content that would resonate with this segment. We pushed out the content and our analytics data indicated more likes and re-posts than at any other time working with this prospect segment. Our next campaign will include input from the siblings, and the university is considering the development of a high school ambassador program."*

WHO Spotting & Response Analysis:

→ Can you see how Jane flipped this into a behavioral question and offered an example to provide evidence?
→ Can you spot the use of WHO Logic in Jane's response?
→ Can you identify how using WHO helps provide proof of value and alignment?

COMMON QUESTIONS

You really can use WHO Logic as a framework to help you with most other questions that come your way. You are demonstrating value and alignment, in the form of examples, often directly from your value points. Let's explore how WHO Logic can help you with responses to a variety of questions.

Jane's Response to a Common Question:

Interviewer: *"Can you share with me your greatest strength?"*

Jane: *"Yes, I am very confident about my communication abilities. I use communication to support others and to influence people. For example, I have served as the student coach and team captain for my club soccer team since my freshman year.*

Last year we had a lot of new members join the team and there were misunderstandings regarding practice and game schedules. Many people showed up at the wrong time and we also missed some games due to not having enough players. Some people were even threatening to quit. I reached out to the new people and asked about communication preferences and how we could make our communication better. I didn't dictate any new methods, I just asked and listened. I took their suggestions to the existing players and convinced them we needed to use a different communication tool for our team. My ability to listen to the new players, to engage them in helping to find a solution, and to convince existing players to adopt the solution demonstrates my communication strengths. We now use WhatsApp, based on the suggestion of our new team members. We have great attendance at our practice sessions and games, and we are building a unified team."

WHO Spotting & Response Analysis:

→ Can you spot the use of WHO Logic in Jane's response?
→ Can you identify how using WHO helps provide proof of value and alignment?

Interviewer
Continues: *"Can you share with me a weakness?"*

Jane: *"Sure, I tend to put too much on my plate, overcommitting sometimes when my schedule is already full. I am making improvements, though, based on some advice I received from my mentor. Every morning, before I start my day, I spend a few minutes analyzing my calendar for the day and the coming weeks. I remind myself of what is due, my priorities and deadlines. I then make a to-do list that I reference throughout the day, every day. By viewing my priorities, I stay focused, and this has helped me learn to say no or defer new opportunities for a later time. This process has become habitual for me. I'm prioritizing and meeting my goals. And this practice has really helped me stay organized and focused, plus the quality of my work has greatly improved."*

WHO Spotting & Response Analysis:

→ Can you spot the use of WHO Logic in Jane's response?
→ Can you identify how using WHO helps provide proof of value and alignment?

Jane's Response to another Common Question:

Interviewer: *"Where do you see yourself in five years?"*

Jane: *"I know I will be working in digital marketing. This is an area where I gravitate and want to continue to grow. I love learning and I want to continue to advance my technical skills, particularly how we use data to understand and predict human behavior to increase market share and profits. I also want to work toward leadership roles where I can support the growth of others and your professional development program at UVW is attractive to me because of the commitment you make to your employees."*

WHO Spotting & Response Analysis:

Jane uses WHO Logic by sharing **what** she will be doing in five years, and she notes **how** she intends to grow in this functional area. She also speaks to her intention to support **outcomes** by helping to increase market share and profits while growing into more progressive roles. She aligns her career progression with UVW's professional development program, asserting an authentic interest in the growth opportunities offered by UVW Corporation.

YOUR CURIOSITY QUESTIONS FOR THE INTERVIEWER

At the end of the interview, the interviewer will typically ask if you have any questions. Use your research. All the WHO inquiry and alignment work you have done in advance of the interview will help you develop curiosity questions. Curiosity questions represent your genuine interest and often relate to **How**.

It's the **How** that is often the unique differentiator for any company. How is tied to action that produces outcomes—value. When you ask curiosity questions connected to **How**, you demonstrate your interest in the value produced by the company *and* you reaffirm your interest in adding value.

Here are some of Jane T. Avatar's **curiosity questions**, primarily anchored in **How:**

→ UVW is using some very innovative practices to produce value. How does marketing fit into the overarching strategy?

→ UVW values entrepreneurialism. How is entrepreneurialism supported and rewarded?

→ UVW has been in the press lately for its work bringing together stakeholders with a strong emphasis on involving consumers in the product design process. How is this going, and will this kind of engagement continue?

→ I noticed the Q3 earnings this past year were 20% higher than the previous year. Is this attributed to the new product launch?

SO MANY POSSIBLE QUESTIONS!

There are many possible questions that can be asked during an interview. The questions Jane T. Avatar received during her interview represent a sample. The objective in sharing Jane's interview is to demonstrate the use of WHO Logic as a structure to help you formulate answers as well as impress upon you how important it is to support your responses by providing examples (evidence).

Given that there are many questions you could be asked during an interview, you can source possible questions and responses using the internet and by gaining insights from people in your network who are affiliated with the company or the industry.

I also suggest that your preparation include flipping the list of responsibilities and qualifications from a job posting into interview questions as part of your interview preparation. For example, if a job posting lists the following responsibilities and qualifications, flip them into interview questions:

RESPONSIBILITIES LISTED IN THE JOB POSTING	Flipped into a question to prepare for the interview
Build a social media campaign	*Do you have experience with social media?*
Use PowerPoint and Excel	*What's your experience using PowerPoint and Excel?*
QUALIFICATIONS LISTED IN THE JOB POSTING	**Flipped into a question to prepare for the interview**
Leadership skills	*Tell me about a time you demonstrated effective leadership?*
Programming languages	*What's your proficiency with different programming languages?*
Persuasive communication	*Tell me about a time you demonstrated persuasive communication?*

Try this: Return to the UVW internship description in Chapter 5 and flip the responsibilities and qualifications into questions.

A FEW FINAL WORDS ABOUT INTERVIEWS... YOU ARE NOT A BOT

Please do not robotize your interview. Don't memorize a bunch of answers for questions that may or may not come your way. Sure, you absolutely can loosely structure your introductory response and you should prepare examples from your experiences (think about your resume value points) to demonstrate relevant skills related to the job. But you need to be open to improvisation, and you must allow your professional personality to shine. Don't be a bot.

AFTER THE INTERVIEW

THANK YOU LETTER(S)

The thank you letter is a must! You need to take time to reflect on the interview, and I recommend sending the thank you within 24–36 hours after the interview. Do give yourself time to assess the experience. Ask yourself, is there anything I want to be sure to emphasize, or that I left out that could further demonstrate my value and alignment?

FIRST ROUND THANK YOU LETTER: SHORT AND FOCUSED

A first round interview is often conducted with a company recruiting representative (someone who does not typically work in the job area) and is typically 20–30 minutes in length. You are often asked to respond to the introductory question, and you will likely have a few conventional and behavioral questions, with more challenging technical questions added the farther along you are in your career. The first round thank you letter is short and focused. You should remind the interviewer(s) of your skills and potential to add value. You should also let the interviewer(s) know you are interested in moving forward. This message is typically sent via email.

Jane's Sample First Round Thank You Letter:

To: mjarian@UVW.com
From: jane.avatar963@gmail.com
Subject: Thank You! (I like exclamation points. Use whatever is comfortable for you.)
Or
Subject: Thank You

Dear Mr. Jarian: Thanks very much for taking time to discuss the marketing internship with me. I enjoyed the conversation and continue to be very interested in this opportunity with UVW. I am confident my digital marketing experience, persuasive communication abilities, and initiative will add value to the company. Please do let me know if you have questions or need additional information from me. I look forward to our next interaction.

Sincerely,
Jane Avatar

SECOND ROUND THANK YOU LETTER: LONGER & MORE CONNECTED

You advanced, so this is getting serious! They like you and you might like them as well. Be observant during the second round. Use what you learned about the role in connection with your skills and experience to articulate value and alignment in the thank you letter.

Jane's Sample Second Round Thank You Letter:

To: jscouter@uvw.com
From: jane.avatar963@gmail.com
Subject: Thank You!

Dear Ms. Scouter:

Thank you for the opportunity to interview for the marketing internship with UVW Corporation. Please extend my thanks to the entire interview committee. I learned a great deal from the conversation and continue to be very interested in the job.

Based on the job posting and our previous discussions, UVW is seeking an individual who has an entrepreneurial mindset, is collaborative, and has skills using technology, with an interest in learning more about innovative practices in digital marketing. Please allow me to reiterate my relevant skills and alignment with the job.

I offer outstanding digital marketing skills based on academic and professional experiences. I intend to build this skill set and would be thrilled to strengthen my technical abilities as an employee with UVW. I have developed strong collaborative relationships resulting in high-performing sales teams. I'm excited about the prospect of working in a highly productive environment where my curiosity and initiative will be supported and rewarded.

Thank you again for sharing time with me. Please let me know if you need additional information or have questions for me. I look forward to hearing from you soon.

Sincerely,
Jane T. Avatar

THIRD ROUND THANK YOU LETTER & BEYOND: SHORT AND FOCUSED

If you have a third round, hold fast with determination and grit. You are on a very short list at this point. The note is short and focused. Jane highlights the value she will gain from the internship along with a declaration of the value she plans to add.

Jane's Sample Third Round Thank You Letter:

To: jscouter@uvw.com
From: jane.avatar963@gmail.com
Subject: Thank You!

Dear Ms. Scouter: Thanks so much for the time you and your team have provided. With each conversation, I become more excited about the possibility of working in the marketing internship. Your willingness to provide mentorship to the successful candidate, along with extensive professional development coaching, are the two most compelling benefits related to this job. If offered, I intend to work hard, learn exponentially, and contribute to the exciting and ambitious goals of the team. I look forward to hearing from you very soon.

Sincerely,
Jane Avatar

OFFER NEGOTIATION

Yes. I'll say it again emphatically: **Yes!** I think you should always negotiate, and I suggest you engage in this important process by way of preparation and substance (i.e., valuation and alignment).

I'm focusing this negotiation segment on the most common negotiated item, salary. However, you can extend the salary negotiation advice to other negotiable items including, but not limited to, benefits, time off, stock options, bonuses, and relocation support.

Your salary negotiation preparation should start with basic data collection. You should review salary data from reliable sources such as a university career services office and/or online sites that specialize in these data. Beyond the act of collecting information, let's continue to explore negotiation by returning to ***buying and selling***. We buy stuff with the idea that the item or service we purchase is equal to or more valuable than the price we pay. If you can remind the employer that they will get tremendous value from you, more value from you than from other options, you might move the dial and receive higher compensation. You must prove your ability to add value, and you do that with evidence. And—there's probably no surprise here—you can use WHO to help you.

INTERNSHIPS & NEGOTIATION

Recall how I asserted that you should always negotiate. Yep, sort of... I do think it's possible to negotiate salary or other associated benefits for an internship, but let's take a brief look at an important attribute of an internship. Internships are just temporary employment, and they are designed with the learner as the primary beneficiary. This is the main reason it's hard to increase the compensation offered for an internship. You are the primary beneficiary of the experience and an employer doesn't expect to get big value from you. You are a learner. Nevertheless, there are times when you may be successful in gaining additional compensation. Based on the job description, in alignment with your skills and experiences, can you guarantee you will add value during this 8- to 16-week period? Use WHO Logic to help you prepare for a negotiation conversation with an internship employer.

→ **WHAT** will you do?
→ **HOW** will you do the work?
→ What specific **OUTCOME(S)** will you produce?

I have worked with many students over the years who have tried to negotiate for additional compensation with an internship employer. I have seen a few students receive a bump in compensation for an internship, but it's rare. Unless you can guarantee significant value will be produced from your work, it's tough to receive more money for an internship experience.

Regardless of your success in this activity, I think negotiating compensation is just good practice. You have spent effort and time assessing your value in relation to the job and company; you understand your value, so you should continue to elevate your valuation practice by articulating and leveraging your value.

One big note here: your request must **be professional, polite, and very respectful**. An employer is giving you an opportunity. You are the learner, and, although you may want to add a tremendous amount of value, your value will likely be limited.

FULL-TIME JOBS & NEGOTIATION

Let me return to my emphatic **Yes!** You must negotiate. To get to this point in the process you have invested in valuation and alignment. You are confident in your potential to add value in this new role, and your skills, experiences, and goals align with the job and company. Negotiation is a declaration of your value. And it's not hard work. The valuation and alignment have been done. So, your preparation is as follows:

A recap of your value based on previous experiences:

→ **WHAT** have you done in the past that aligns with the job?
→ **HOW** have you completed the work?
→ What specific **OUTCOME(S)** have you produced?

A declaration of the value you intend to add:

→ **WHAT** will you do?
→ **HOW** will you do the work?
→ What specific **OUTCOME(S)** will you produce?

These are things you have likely already shared during the interview. Do it again, politely, pleasantly, and with respect. Remind your future employer of your value. People respond to repetition, recall, and elevated practice. Pleasantly and assertively share your value and politely ask for more money and/or other benefits you seek.

As appropriate, share comparative compensation data from reliable sources, particularly if the salary and compensation offered to you is low relative to the prevailing wage.

The employer will rarely give you exactly what you suggest, which is why you should aim higher than what you will ultimately accept. The negotiation continues until an agreement happens. Sometimes it's just impossible for the employer to budge, and it's at this point that you must decide if the existing offer works for you.

A FEW ADDITIONAL TIPS ON NEGOTIATION

Engage in this conversation verbally, most commonly on the phone. This is not an email exchange. You can certainly request a meeting by email, but aim for having the conversation on the phone.

If you are requesting a meeting by email, use something like the following message:

Dear [insert name, typically HR recruiter or hiring manager]: I am pleased to receive the offer of employment with [name of company]. I do have questions regarding compensation and I am wondering if you have time within the next day or two to chat with me.

Thank you,
[Your Name]

THE NEGOTIATION CONVERSATION

You can frame the conversation as follows:

→ Thank the company for the opportunity and share your sincere interest in the job.

→ Remind them of the conversation topic: you would like to discuss compensation.

→ Share any data you have gathered regarding average salary for the role; include cost-of-living estimates and any other supportive data related to salary or other forms of compensation.

→ Remind the organization of the value you bring based on past experiences, skills, and any new skills you may be adding (recent training, degree completion, or other relevant professional development).

→ Ask if they can get you closer to $X (use the high end of the range based on your research).

→ If you are negotiating for something other than salary, (benefits, signing bonus, other forms of compensation), politely make the ask.

→ Be ready to move back and forth in conversation until you finally settle on something agreeable to both parties (you may have many conversations over several days/weeks).

→ Once the final offer is received, you will need to determine if you want to accept or decline it.

NO OFFER? NO WORRIES

Maybe you didn't get the offer. It's okay when this happens. This is not an *if*, it's a *when*. Recall Chapter 8 and the Jane T. Avatar scenario where she was the best on paper but others out-networked her and Jane didn't move on to the interview round. This can happen with offers as well. Sometimes another candidate may have stronger connections and endorsements. You perform better in the interview and the other candidate still receives the offer. This happens. It's real. Sometimes the best candidate doesn't get the job.

Sometimes you don't make the case for value and alignment. That happens, too. If you aren't selected, pick yourself up, dust off, and move on. Grit is important here.

This rejection thing can go both ways. Sometimes you will receive an offer and reject the opportunity. The fit isn't right, the salary is low, and the employer will not budge; perhaps you are waiting on another option. It runs both ways.

CHAPTER END & NEXT UP

This chapter represents the culmination of using WHO Logic specifically as a market readiness tool for all actions associated with networking and the job search. My hope is that you are thinking about value more than you were prior to reading the book and that you are able to confidently assess, articulate, and leverage your value in alignment with the direction in which you are headed.

As previously mentioned, you will want to stay market ready, for promotions, raises, and opportunities at companies where you are employed, and when you seek advancement elsewhere.

We're moving into a deeper form of market readiness—career advancement. Networking continues. Hard work and engagement in your projects and tasks continue. Valuation? Yep, it's more important than ever.

10

Career Management

To Fully Engage in Internships & Other Applied Learning Experiences

Welcome to Chapter 10! We're moving into career advancement, an extension of market readiness. Yes, you will want to stay market ready throughout your career, not because you are perpetually looking for a new job, but because you are learning, growing, and likely seeking advancement with an existing employer as well as staying open to external opportunities.

Following our friend Jane T. Avatar, the logical next step in her advancement is an internship. WHO Logic is coming along with us on this journey, because valuation continues to be a critical part of career management.

INTERNSHIPS & OTHER APPLIED LEARNING EXPERIENCES

Please don't let the term *internship* deceive you. I can't tell you the number of students I have worked with who are obsessed with the idea that the experience must be called an internship. The idea that something labeled "internship" is more valuable than other applied learning experiences is just not true. Yes, an internship can help you build skills and land full-time employment, but so can other experiences. Here's the thing: internships are just temporary employment, so please don't get caught up in the term. I use the word *internship* in the book because it's a recognizable term, but valuable experiences come with many different titles.

Part-time jobs, volunteering, internships, and other related skill-building activities fall under the broad umbrella of **common applied learning experiences** (fig. 11). All can be valuable, valued, and leveraged. Please don't forget that experience matters, but the experience doesn't have to be called an internship. That's why you see the long chapter title, because applied learning experiences matter. Anything that helps you build skills and add value to an organization matters, particularly if the skills and value-add are connected to the direction you are headed in.

COMMON APPLIED LEARNING EXPERIENCES

Volunteering
Internships
Part-Time Jobs
Research
Travel/Study Abroad
Athletics/Club Involvement

fig. 11

Let's return to Jane T. Avatar and her career advancement journey. She has accepted a marketing internship from UVW Corporation. It's important to note that an internship is designed to focus on the advancement of the learner (aka the student), meaning that the company should not expect to gain significant value from the outputs of the intern.

Although Jane wants to make a great impact, the learning is the focus. However, the assessment of value, alignment, and fit certainly continues. Sometimes an internship can be similar to a long-term applied interview. Why? Because hiring is an expensive and risky business, so an internship is a great way for the company (and for the intern) to assess value, alignment, and fit, and to answer the question, *"Do we want to turn this internship into a permanent role when the time is right?"*

Not all companies use internships as extended interviews with the goal of converting a portion of the interns into full-time permanent hires. Some merely need to get work done, while providing a learning opportunity for students with no intention of full-time conversion.

When you are headed into an internship, please know that you do have the opportunity to add value, but it's possible you will not be there long enough to see actual outcomes associated with your labor. It's also possible that your internship outputs may not be used. Both situations are okay. In terms of assessing and articulating the value of an internship, valuation is focused more on intended outcomes than actual outcomes. And sometimes the outcomes are more about your skill enhancement, given that the primary beneficiary of an internship is you, the learner. So, the value of an internship is often focused on **skill enhancement** and **intended outcomes**.

CURIOSITY IS AT THE CORE OF YOUR INTERNSHIP

Let curiosity lead as you navigate the new environment. Ask questions, immerse yourself in the company, learn the culture, understand the values, take initiative, and deploy your growth mindset. Be intentional with your role.

Let's look at how you can maximize your internship using WHO to support your learning and valuation efforts. We'll then explore how Jane T. Avatar fully engages in her applied learning experience.

FULLY ENGAGING IN YOUR INTERNSHIP/APPLIED LEARNING EXPERIENCE

The internship begins and you are at the company site for a period that is typically 8–14 weeks in length. You spend the first week or more onboarding. Onboarding, or orientation, is critically important. It's an introduction to the culture, business unit, and job. Onboarding also serves to provide you with information, resources, and tools you will need to work on projects and tasks.

Your onboarding could be extensive or rather sparse. Don't despair if your onboard is minimal or nonexistent. If minimal, this just means you may have to take initiative to obtain the information, resources, and tools you need. Internships and applied learning experiences are varied, so you may need to ask more questions than you anticipated.

Pay attention during onboarding, particularly to information about strategy: the What, How, and Outcomes related to the company and the functional unit in which you work. Understanding strategy for both the company and the functional unit is important because of valuation.

You want to be engaged in work that elevates your skills and adds value to the organization. You will likely be evaluated by a supervisor, and just like variances in onboarding, internship evaluations vary by company. Some evaluations are very constructive with interactive and rich feedback, and some are minimal without much depth. Regardless, it's important for you to engage in valuation regarding your learning and the impact your efforts have in relation to business unit and/or company strategy. After all, it's you who will ultimately tell the story about this experience.

WHAT IS STRATEGY?

Very simply stated, strategy at a for-profit company is the "to-do" list for making money and creating value. Strategy at a not-for-profit company is the "to-do" list for creating and offering value.

The WHO framework offers a simple option for thinking about strategy:

Strategy Simplification using WHO (For-Profit Companies)

→ **W** = **WHAT** does the company do to make money and create value? *(product and/or service)*

→ **H** = **HOW** does the company make money and create value? *(strategic actions, methods, innovations)*

→ **O** = Intended or Actual **OUTCOMES** produced? *(related to value and profit)*

Strategy Simplification using WHO (Not-For-Profit Companies)

→ **W** = **WHAT** does the organization do to create value? *(product and/or service)*

→ **H** = **HOW** does the organization create value? *(strategic actions, methods, innovations)*

→ **O** = Intended or Actual **OUTCOMES** produced? *(value creation related to improved lives, communities, and resources)*

Let's illustrate the connection between strategy and the internship experience by inserting Jane T. Avatar into the conversation. Jane is headed to UVW for a summer marketing internship.

We now find Jane in the first week at UVW, amid onboarding, and here are a few of her notes from the company and the marketing unit orientation.

JANE T. AVATAR'S NOTES: FIRST WEEK

May 17 – Onboarding Meeting, Led by Matt Jarian – Intern Onboarding Coordinator

Company Overview:

UVW – History. They have been around since 1945 as regional staffing firm, turned national and now global as of 1990. Viewed as leaders in anticipating labor trends and needs in the workforce. Expanded in 2009 to provide upskill training to meet changing demands of workforce. Another expansion in 2019, training on market readiness and career advancement through a subsidiary company referred to as WHO Logic.

My simplified strategy for UVW using WHO

W = What do they do? Talent solutions company. UVW matchmakes talent with companies; offers additional value-add services including upskill training, market readiness, and career advancement training.

H = How do they do the work? Conduct labor trend research; develop and maintain outstanding relationships with companies – focus on customer experience, nimble – accurate forecasting of labor trends and needs; they value innovation and curiosity with a start-up feel – entrepreneurial culture.

O = Outcomes? Leader in the staffing services market. $$ Net Profit = 30% higher year over year than closest competitor.

Marketing Unit Overview: (the functional area of my internship)

My simplified strategy for the Marketing Unit using WHO

W = What does this unit do? Focus is on the customer experience. Promote staffing services, lead relationship-building strategies with account managers. Promote upskill training. Taking on promotion of new market readiness and career advancement subsidiary.

H = How does the unit do the work? Market research, deploy unique customer experience tools and techniques, serve as the "skunk works" unit within the company – the prototyping unit.

O = Outcomes Produced? Innovation central, contribute to net profits, keep organization top-of-mind for existing and potential customers.

May 19, My Main Project – Distributed by Jill Scouter, Customer Experience Director

Assigned to work on the new training service offered through the subsidiary, WHO Logic.

W = What will I do to support this project? Market Research - feasibility for market readiness and career advancement training to be offered as an option for existing customers and explore potential to expand customer base to include colleges and universities.

H = How will I do the work? By using survey and analytics tools to collect and analyze data regarding existing customer base and potential new customer segment.

O = Intended Outcomes? For the company: Use data to inform UVW of potential value-add for existing customer base and viability of expanding into a new customer base. Outcomes for me: develop deeper skills with surveying and analytics tools, expansion of existing customer base into new product/service, exploration of new customer segment with a new product/service.

Jane's notes will help her develop a better understanding of how the internship experience adds value to the company and the marketing unit, and she can measure her learning and value-add in alignment with the business strategy and outcomes.

If you find yourself in an internship and the outcomes, goals, and strategic actions are not shared, ask to see the strategic plan or the business plan. If this information isn't available, ask your supervisor to clarify the goals and strategic actions of the business unit and company. If your supervisor is unable to articulate the goals and actions, use the WHO framework to devise a simplified strategy, then share this information with your supervisor to determine if you have accurately interpreted the strategy/goals of the business unit and company. It's important for you to link your learning and value to strategy and outcomes. Why? It's an important part of your story. The experience has more value if you can demonstrate how your work aligned with the organization's strategy and outcomes.

NETWORKING OPPORTUNITIES WITH YOUR INTERNSHIP EMPLOYER!

Need a refresher on the value of networking? Revisit Chapter 8. Recall that networking goes beyond securing a job. Your network is an important part of lifelong career advancement.

Be an adventurer! Plan to network beyond your immediate circle of colleagues. Talk with people outside your assigned unit. Use curiosity to explore, learn, and expand your network.

Once your projects and tasks begin, you will continue to learn more about company culture as each day progresses. You will engage in internal networking by interacting with people who work at the company both in your functional unit and beyond.

In addition to learning more about company culture and engaging in networking, you should expect to enhance skills, including job-related technical skills, while also adding value to the company. There is a lot going on for you to evaluate!

You will need to engage in reflection and assessment of the experience, i.e., valuation. WHO Logic provides a great framework for a regular *Valuation Practice*.

The Valuation Practice helps you reflect and assess:

→ your learning
→ the value you are adding to the company
→ your interest and potential for work within the functional area
→ your interest and potential for work at this company

VALUATION PRACTICE – INTRODUCTION TO
THE DAILY WHO-5, WEEKLY WHO-15 & FINAL WHO-30

WHO LOGIC FOR INTERNSHIP VALUATION. Using WHO Logic for internship valuation will help you assess your learning and uncover value. I recommend daily and weekly short valuation reflection and assessment periods with a final valuation to comprehensively evaluate the experience.

The remainder of the chapter includes an overview of the daily, weekly, and final WHO valuation practice and an example of the process by way of Jane T. Avatar and her internship with UVW Corporation.

THE DAILY WHO-5
(Daily 5-Minute Reflection and Assessment Practice Using WHO Logic)

At the end of the day, spend 5 minutes reflecting and assessing. It's simple and quick. Stay true to the 5-minute time allocation. This is not supposed to be onerous, just quick reflection and assessment.

Be economical. Your daily WHO-5 is quick valuation. Value is defined as value to your learning and value to the company. Move through WHO Logic; then rate engagement, learning, the culture, and your networking.

By conducting WHO-5s, you are generating lots of information, including a list of tasks and activities along with skills and intended outcomes. The daily WHO-5 experience is meant to be generative. You are collecting lots of data, to then analyze and reduce, helping you move forward to your final assessment.

JANE T. AVATAR – **INTERN @ UVW: DAILY WHO-5**

Project: Market Research – feasibility for career management training to be offered as an option for existing customers and exploration of possible new market – colleges and universities.

Inventory and Evaluate Your Experience Today, 3 Minutes:

WHAT did I do? *(1–3 tasks)*	Task 1 – What: Built draft survey for existing clientele Task 2 – What: Gathered demographic information for college-age students in the U.S.
HOW did I do the work? *(skills, technical tools, methods)*	Task 1 – How: Reviewed new service and subsidiary company, explored Google Forms to familiarize, independently created survey questions Task 2 – How: Extracted data from National Center for Education Statistics
OUTCOMES? *(intended, actual, learning)*	Task 1 – Outcomes: Completed draft survey for review by marketing team and customer experience director, increased proficiency with Google Forms and data analytics Task 2 – Outcomes: Generated data to support next steps in market analysis

Rate Your Experience Today & Networking Quick Notes, 2 Minutes:

Rating	Poor	Fair	Average	Good	Good+	Excellent	N/A
My Engagement					X		
My Learning					X		
Culture/People					X		
Networking/People						X	

Networking Quick Notes:

(Use the space below to make a few notes. Think about the people you interacted with today and who you want to build a relationship with over time; include names and titles.)

Bernadette Velguth, Customer Experience Associate Director – very helpful, provided advice and shared her professional background. Danielle Alex, Data Analyst – spent time demonstrating analytics tools and offered to provide additional coaching.

THE WEEKLY WHO-15

(Weekly 15-Minute Reflection and Assessment Practice Using WHO Logic)

At the end of each week, take 5 minutes to review your daily WHO-5 outputs for the entire week. **Select the most valuable task or activity.** Value is determined by value to your learning and value to the company.

Use the next 10 minutes to apply WHO Logic for the valuation; then rate your engagement and learning, the culture, and your networking.

JANE T. AVATAR – **INTERN @ UVW: WEEKLY WHO-15**

Select the most valuable and valued task from the week, 5 Minutes.
Assess the task, 5 Minutes:

WHAT did I do? *(most valued task/activity)*	Most Valued Task: Created and administered needs and interest survey
HOW did I do the work? *(skills, technical tools, methods)*	How: Using Google Forms, collaborated with the team to obtain input for question development
OUTCOMES? *(intended, actual, learning)*	Outcome: Analyzed data from 35K respondents and generated insights to affirm high probability of sales from existing clientele

Rate Your Experience This Week & Networking Quick Notes, 5 Minutes:

Rating	Poor	Fair	Average	Good	Good+	Excellent	N/A
My Engagement						X	
My Learning					X		
Culture/People					X		
Networking/People						X	

Networking Quick Notes:
(Use the space below to make a few notes. Think about the people you interacted with this week and who you want to build a relationship with over time; include names, titles, and other interesting information.)

Garth Rodriguez, Director of Sales – coffee chat. Discussed his background and received valuable advice on networking and continuous learning ideas. Helen Mac, Talent Developer – great advice on professional associations and conference options for this field.

THE FINAL WHO-30

(Final Reflection and Assessment Practice Using WHO Logic)

At the end of your internship, take 10 minutes to review your weekly WHO-15 outputs. Select up to five of the most valuable tasks or activities connected to your entire internship experience. Remember, value is determined by value to your learning and value to the company.

Use the next 20 minutes to apply WHO Logic for the valuation; then rate your engagement and learning, the culture, and your networking.

Review Your WHO-15 Outputs, 10 Minutes. Select up to five most valuable and valued tasks/ activities during your entire internship. Assess the tasks/activities, 10 Minutes:

WHAT did I do? *(up to 5 tasks/activities)*	Task 1 – What: Created and administered needs and interests survey Task 2 – What: Led a focus group of 22 company-wide peer interns, assessed their interest in valuation training Task 3 – What: Created the presentation supporting the service expansion to existing and new markets
HOW did I do the work? *(skills, technical tools, methods)*	Task 1 – How: Using Google Forms, collaborated with team for input Task 2 – How: Built focus group questions, analyzed data Task 3 – How: Utilized Tableau and PowerPoint and created sophisticated graphics to highlight data and insights
OUTCOMES? *(intended, actual, learning)*	Task 1 – Outcomes: Analyzed data from 35K respondents, generated insights to affirm high probability of sales from existing clientele Task 2 – Outcomes: Offered insights to marketing and customer experience team Task 3 – Outcomes: To support the sales potential for the new service with existing and new market, presented to C-Suite
Strategy and Value Alignment	Strategic Target for UVW – Expansion into new service delivery line. Value Alignment of my project: Added a comprehensive data set to reinforce sales potential

Rate Your Entire Experience & Quick Notes, 10 Minutes:

Rating	Poor	Fair	Average	Good	Good+	Excellent	N/A
My Engagement					X		
My Learning						X	
Culture/People					X		
Networking/People						X	
Could I Launch My Career Here?					X		

Networking Quick Notes:
(Use the space below to make a few notes. Include names and titles of people you want to build a relationship with over time. Answer the following question: could I launch my career here? Why or why not?)

Plan to build relationships with all individuals listed in daily and weekly WHO valuation. Yes, I could launch my career with UVW. Professional development opportunities are abundant. Creativity and out-of-the-box thinking are highly valued. People are friendly and work-life balance is supported. There are also free snacks offered throughout the day and an on-site gym!

BEYOND YOUR FINAL REFLECTION
& ASSESSMENT PRACTICE USING WHO LOGIC

Now what? What do you do with all this information? So much!

The final WHO reflection and assessment will help generate your resume value points, giving you new evidence in the form of examples (stories) for marketing yourself. Your WHO reflection and assessment results might also influence your ever-evolving value proposition and conversational pitch.

Additional outcomes of your internship valuation practice include rating your engagement, learning, the culture, and your networking. Your ratings help you evaluate whether the work is of interest to you.

Rating results from observations of the culture and your networking activity help you determine if this could be a good place to start your career. Ratings also help you determine if the company employs people you would like to continue to build relationships with, people who might offer mentorship, and people you can support and add value to over time.

The engagement, learning, culture, and networking can be very interrelated. If, for example, the people aren't great and the networking was essentially nonexistent, this type of environment can put a damper on your engagement and learning. Culture matters. People matter. So, view your final assessment holistically.

Keep your WHO valuation data. This information is a record of your applied learning experience, valuable as you continue to grow and advance professionally. It's like a journal or diary, fun and informative to use in the moment and incredibly revealing as time and your career progress.

CHAPTER END & NEXT UP

Most companies have some form of internship evaluation. If so, that's great. Use what is available to you. Make sure the valuation practice is one that offers the opportunity for reflection and assessment related to your learning and the value you add to the organization. Incorporate WHO Logic as you deem appropriate and useful.

One of the best outcomes associated with continued use of WHO Logic is sticky learning! Because you use WHO as your primary valuation tool throughout market readiness and career advancement activities, the repetition, recall, and elevated practice result in deep and sticky learning of valuation, a critical part of lifelong career management. The WHO Mindset forms and sticks!

Chapter 11 brings us to our final career education chapter. The focus is on managing and advancing your career, keeping in mind three important components: smart work, valuation, and networking—with an emphasis on valuation. The journey continues, and along for the ride is your growing valuation mindset that uses a very simple yet robust logic framework to support lifelong career advancement: WHO Logic.

Let's see how...

11

Career Management
To Fully Engage in Career Advancement

Chapter 10 demonstrated how to use WHO as an on-the-job valuation tool for applied learning experiences. We move along in our journey, elevating the practice of valuation using WHO Logic to support your progression as a full-time, career advancing employee regardless of industry sector and whether you're progressing in for-profit companies, not-for-profit organizations, government, education or any other entity whereby you work to add value. And we'll place even more emphasis on aligning your work with strategy, important throughout all phases of your career—early, mid, and advanced.

There's a lot going on in this chapter, so let's engage in a quick overview. The first segment of Chapter 11 includes the introduction to what I believe are the three "essentials" necessary for career advancement, then we'll merge these essentials with several valuation approaches to career advancement. I will share a reminder about the importance of aligning your work with strategy, setting up for the final segment: a return to our friend Jane T. Avatar who will help actualize WHO Logic for career advancement.

ESSENTIALS FOR CAREER ADVANCEMENT –
SMART WORK, VALUATION, AND NETWORKING

Allow me to set the stage for the use of WHO Logic by introducing three essential ingredients for career success: *smart work*, *valuation*, and *networking*.

Smart Work: Working hard on the job and working strategically on relevant, aligned projects and initiatives that map to the success targets and metrics of the organization. Smart work also means investing in training, education, and continuous learning, necessary for building and sustaining your career.

Valuation & Alignment: The ability to assess your smart work, generate evidence of value, and confidently articulate and leverage your value to obtain raises, promotions, and opportunities (with an existing employer or new company). The ability to align your smart work and value with the next move in your career.

Networking: Relationship-building with people who are working in jobs of interest at the existing company (where you work) or external companies (where you may want to work). We typically don't advance on our own. Most of us advance by way of collaboration and support.

CAREER ADVANCEMENT AND THE PASSIVE APPROACH

Let's examine the connection between the three essentials and career advancement by returning to several valuation approaches introduced in Chapter 1.

Recall the ***passive career advancement approach***. The value you produce is readily noticed and rewarded. The process is basically this: Your work adds value, your employer carefully evaluates and rewards your efforts; raises, promotions and career advancement opportunities come to you by way of *their* careful assessment of your value (fig. 12).

fig. 12 ▼

The challenge with the passive approach is that decision makers may not carefully assess the value you add. The passive approach assumes your value will be regularly measured and rewarded.

For example, here's a perfectly fine scenario demonstrating the passive career advancement approach: It's the 18-month mark of your new job. Your boss comes to you and says, "I have been evaluating your efforts in alignment with our outcomes and you have been hitting the target at every benchmark. It's time for your performance-based raise and promotion." Your boss pays very close attention to your value-add; focuses on your growth, raises, and promotions; and develops opportunities for you.

This scenario would be nice and does happen, but not that often; and do you really want someone else to own your valuation and career advancement?

CAREER ADVANCEMENT AND THE ACTIVE APPROACH

By developing a WHO Mindset, you take much more ownership of your career advancement. Through valuation, you regularly assess, articulate, and leverage the value of your work, generating evidence that can be used for negotiating salary and advancement with an existing employer or in the open labor market. Adopting the WHO Mindset supports an active career advancement approach (fig. 13).

fig. 13 ▼

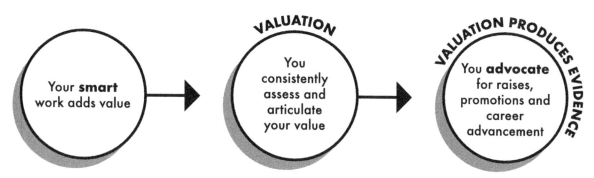

CAREER ADVANCEMENT & A MORE ACTIVE APPROACH

There is yet another action necessary with this more active approach. You need **networking**—internal and external networking to build relationships and advocates who will endorse and support your advancement, because we typically do not advance independently of others (fig. 14).

fig. 14 ▼

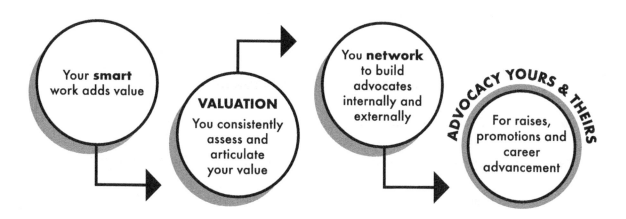

ALIGNING YOUR SMART WORK WITH COMPANY STRATEGY

Before launching into the practical and tactical use of WHO Logic for career advancement, let's pause for a reminder. We all work on tasks that aren't directly related to the intended and actual outcomes of an organization or business unit. I'm not advising you to engage in valuation for everything you do, just your most value-centered tasks. Be judicious. Remember to prioritize work that is most connected to strategic actions, goals, and outcomes. Ask yourself with every task, how important is this to strategy?

STRATEGY THROUGH THE WHO LOGIC LENS

Let's return to strategy for just a moment, because developing and deploying strategy is all about reaching the goal: generating profit and creating value.

Simply stated, strategy at a for-profit company includes the strategic actions (How) for making money and creating value. Strategy at a not-for-profit company includes the strategic actions (How) for creating and offering value. Strategy is also tied to outcomes. Outcomes are associated with money made, value created. It's that simple.

Organizations exist to create value, and within an organization, all functional units exist to support the creation of value.

The WHO framework offers a simple option for thinking about strategy at a very macro level:

Strategy Simplification Using WHO *(For-Profit Companies)*

→ **W** = **WHAT** does the company do to make money and create value? *(product and/or service)*

→ **H** = **HOW** does the company make money and create value? *(strategic actions, methods, innovations)*

→ **O** = Intended and Actual **OUTCOMES** produced? *(related to value and profit)*

Strategy Simplification Using WHO *(Not-For-Profit Companies)*

→ **W** = **WHAT** does the organization do to create value? *(product and/or service)*

→ **H** = **HOW** does the organization create value? *(strategic actions, methods, innovations)*

→ **O** = Intended and Actual **OUTCOMES** produced? *(value creation related to improved lives, communities, and resources)*

WORKING FOR YOUR RESUME

I often refer to continuous market readiness and career advancement as "working for your resume." The idea is that you are analyzing and shaping your work in alignment with where you are headed professionally while strategically adding value along the way. Do you have that much control, to shape your work? Yes, I believe you do. Behave like an entrepreneur or business owner in your role and you might be surprised at how much control you have. Understand what the organization cares about and strategically add value.

CAREER ADVANCEMENT VALUATION PRACTICE USING WHO LOGIC

Like the internship valuation practice introduced in Chapter 10, WHO Logic can be deployed to help you reflect and assess your full-time, career-centered work. Consistent outputs from a WHO Logic valuation practice provide important evidence to use as leverage for compensation increases, promotions, and new opportunities.

THERE ARE THREE STEPS IN THE CAREER ADVANCEMENT VALUATION PRACTICE

→ Step 1: Career Advancement Valuation Practice – *Map Your Job*
→ Step 2: Career Advancement Valuation Practice – *The Weekly 20 Minute WHO Assessment*
→ Step 3: Career Advancement Valuation Practice – *Comprehensive Checkups*

STEP 1: CAREER ADVANCEMENT VALUATION PRACTICE — MAP YOUR JOB

You must first align your job with the business unit and company strategy. How do you align? First, you map.

Mapping provides a framework, a structure to keep you on path. Please allow me to share a little bit of health and wellness advice—when you are new on the job, mapping is an important activity. Early in your role you should work toward understanding how your job aligns (maps) with strategy and impacts business unit and company outcomes. I advise you to engage in this early-in-the-role understanding while at the same time urging you to take time to learn! You shouldn't begin a job with an overly aggressive goal of adding big value right away. You need time to acclimate and learn. Most companies don't expect return on the hiring investment right away. Give yourself time.

Mapping helps you understand how your work aligns to the company goals and outcomes (strategy). Review your map regularly given that business plans often change, and your role can change, too. Anyone can map at any time.

Don't map in isolation! Talk with your team, and most importantly, talk with your supervisor. Gain clarity on the strategy and your job. Use your curiosity, commitment to learning, and passion for challenge to understand how your job aligns with the business unit and company strategy.

Let's put a framework around the mapping and call on Jane T. Avatar to serve as our example.

Our story has advanced, and Jane T. Avatar has accepted a full-time role as a digital marketing specialist with UVW. She's in her first three months on the job and has long since completed orientation and initial training. She works in the Marketing and Customer Experience Unit where she was an intern, and she is the junior digital marketing specialist within the unit.

Jane spent time in her first few months at UVW aligning her role with the company and the business unit's strategic actions and intended outcomes. Here is a sample from her alignment and mapping, reviewed and supported by her supervisor.

Jane T. Avatar's Map

SELECT LIST OF JANE'S RESPONSIBILITIES MAPPED TO UVW STRATEGIC PLAN	SELECT OUTCOMES FROM THE UVW STRATEGIC PLAN
	(Jane selects the intended outcomes from the strategic plan that align with her job)

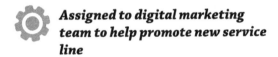
Assigned to digital marketing team to help promote new service line

1. Increase company growth by 4% above previous year ➤ ⚙⚙⚙

2. Increase company revenues by 20% above previous year ➤ ⚙⚙⚙

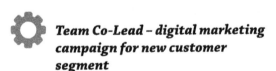
Team Co-Lead – digital marketing campaign for new customer segment

3. Launch new service line with 70% usage from existing customers and 30% usage from new market ➤ ⚙⚙

4. New service line revenue generation target for first year launch: 3% ➤ ⚙⚙

Work within team to expand digital footprint – outreach & relationship development campaigns

5. Expand digital marketing reach to 4 million new followers across Facebook, Twitter and Instagram ➤ ⚙⚙⚙

STEP 2: CAREER ADVANCEMENT VALUATION PRACTICE — THE WEEKLY 20-MINUTE WHO ASSESSMENT

Jane will use this map to support her weekly valuation practice.

STEP 3: CAREER ADVANCEMENT VALUATION PRACTICE — COMPREHENSIVE CHECKUPS

To complement the 20-minute weekly valuation, **_Comprehensive Checkups_** are advised. Best uses for checkups: mapping adjustments, resume updates, leverage, and visioning.

JANE T. AVATAR'S WEEKLY AND COMPREHENSIVE WHO VALUATION PRACTICE

CAREER ADVANCEMENT VALUATION PRACTICE – **WEEKLY WHO-20**

Select the most valued projects/tasks for the week and use WHO Logic to evaluate

WHAT did I do? *(most valued projects/tasks)*	Most Valued Projects/Tasks: New customer segment development. Introduced valuation as a career management tool for college student population (17–25 age range)
HOW did I do the work? *(skills, technical tools, methods)*	How: Campaign targets – Obtained Facebook, Twitter, and Instagram demographic and behavioral data. Lead developer of the WHO are you campaign
OUTCOMES? *(intended, actual, learning)*	Outcomes: Actual Outcome: WHO Logic website hits grew from zero to 1 million within 60 days of campaign launch Intended Outcome: College students purchase apps and associated services from the WHO Logic product line

Map Your WHO Outcomes to UVW Strategy:

Actual Outcome:

WHO Logic website hits grew from zero to 1 million within 60 days of campaign launch. My outcome maps most specifically to UVW Outcomes 3 and 5.

Intended Outcome:

College students purchase apps and associated services from the WHO Logic product line. My outcome maps generally to UVW Outcomes 1, 2, and 4.

Rate Your Experience:

Rating	Poor	Fair	Average	Good	Good+	Excellent	N/A
My Engagement					X		
Learning & Professional Growth						X	
Culture/People						X	
Networking/People				X			
Interjections		X					

Comments:

Strong engagement but was pulled into a few other marketing unit projects this week and didn't meet some of my intended goals. Valuable support from seasoned colleagues who helped me with the campaign theme — WHO are you? Love my colleagues! Not as much company-wide networking as I would like given the pace of the week. Will aim for a coffee with one of the business development managers next week.

INTERJECTIONS AND PROFESSIONAL GROWTH

Note that the Weekly Career Advancement Valuation Practice includes some category changes in the rating grid. The *Interjections* category has been introduced as a means to document interruptions during the week. For example, were you pulled into several unplanned meetings or situations, did you need to work on urgent tasks for your boss, colleagues, or others who influence your work, did you experience other interruptions deviating you from your work objectives for the week?

The Interjections category is important. Today's world of work moves fast, and we are often bombarded with tasks that aren't necessarily connected to our own specific priorities. That's fine and to be expected, but if you notice that you have a continued rating of "poor" for the Interjections category, you may wish to begin deeper documentation. Stuff happens, and there are times when you must set your priorities aside for the good of the business unit or company. However, for you to succeed on the job, you require time to do the job.

I might suggest that interjections are a significant challenge for most folks. Part of our interjected world has to do with the pace of work (everything seems urgent); the other interjection influence is the sheer quantity of information that turns into work, work that may not be critical to the goal.

If you find yourself working in a world of too many interjections, the situation is likely not sustainable, and you will need to do something. **Negotiate.** Please know that it isn't enough to go to your supervisor and simply state that you are overworked. However, something does have to give, because working significantly more than the typical work week (40-ish hours) is likely not the answer. You must see yourself as a partner in this challenge, and you will need to offer evidence and possible solutions.

Return to your map. Review your regular WHO valuations. Meet with your supervisor and remind this person of your priorities in relation to company and business unit outcomes. Use your data and evidence to formulate and offer solutions. Perhaps priorities need to change. Perhaps some of your existing tasks or projects need to be replaced with more pressing tasks, even temporarily. Engage your supervisor in this situation and collaborate toward a solution.

Professional growth has also been added to the Learning category, to encourage your reflection on training and development needs. Do you need additional skills or tools to add value to the company and to support your growth?

If your WHO valuation and ratings are generally positive, you are likely in growth mode. If not, you can use this information to help you engage in productive conversations with a supervisor. Yes, your ratings are subjective but useful to support emotion-neutral, solutions-driven discussions.

Using the outputs from your valuation practice, you generate evidence of value that has been mapped to strategy, and you can leverage this evidence as needed.

CAREER ADVANCEMENT VALUATION PRACTICE – COMPREHENSIVE VALUATION CHECKUP

Your comprehensive valuation checkup occurs every 3–6 months for about 60 minutes. Let's look at Jane T. Avatar's checkup.

Jane T. Avatar, Digital Marketing Specialist – Comprehensive Valuation Checkup:

Review company and business unit strategy:

Quarter 3 reduction in revenue target – from 20% to 18% based on macro changes in the labor market impacting existing service lines.

> Note changes and make any adjustments in mapping.

Review your weekly WHO-20 data:

The "WHO are you?" campaign is huge. Reached annual target to expand to 4 M new users across social media and hit this target within 6 months of launch.

New Target Market (college students) - Conversions from social media followers to engagement and sales; established baseline – met and exceeded monthly and quarterly targets. Increased revenues.

> What pops to the surface? Where is your big value? What outcomes matter the most, to the company and to you? What can you leverage – for raises, promotions, new opportunities?

Successfully supported market research team by generating insights and analytics for "WHO are you?" campaign – proven performer in data analysis. Seeking more time in this space. Secured advocacy from team lead.

Won company "Newcomer Award" for demonstrating entrepreneurial mindset.

Visioning:

What are your entrepreneurial ideas and opportunities for adding value – to the company, for yourself?

WHAT will I do?	Projects/Tasks: Customize our primary analytics tool to filter data on a more granular level
HOW will I do the work?	How: Work directly with the software provider to build out additional filtering options
OUTCOMES?	Intended Outcomes: Expand our knowledge set for deeper market segmentation, develop more personalized advertising to increase sales and company growth

Review Your Weekly Ratings and Aggregate for each Category:

Rating	Poor	Fair	Average	Good	Good+	Excellent	N/A
My Engagement					X		
Learning & Professional Growth					X		
Culture/People						X	
Networking/People				X			
Interjections	X						

Comments:

Exciting outputs and outcomes. I have much to leverage and will be using the evidence I have produced to negotiate my second raise since starting in the role 9 months ago. My biggest challenge has to do with the amount of interjection I face. I am drawn into many projects external and internal to the marketing unit. Great opportunity to work across functional units and in different areas within my unit (particularly market research) but making it tough to stay on top of my own priorities in relation to company and unit outcomes.

Next week's one-on-one with my boss, I will share my understanding of my priorities in relation to company and business unit outcomes. I will present several solutions to the interjection challenge, including spending a bit more time with research and analytics using data to support the rationale for eliminating or at least reducing some of my current responsibilities.

External networking is going well. I'm involved in several early-professional "after 5" networking groups and one professional association. My internal networking is not as productive as I would like, but I have regular conversations with aspirational individuals – people I want to be...

WEEKLY WHOS, COMPREHENSIVE CHECKUPS AND CONTINUED MARKET READINESS

The timing I recommend for engaging in WHO Valuation Practice and WHO Valuation Checkups is really your decision. For some, weekly valuation may be best, and for others a monthly valuation practice is ideal. Whatever you choose, be sure to include an annual or semiannual comprehensive checkup. It's your valuation practice. You decide what works best for you. Just be sure you engage in some form of valuation to help you chart your career advancement journey. Valuation will also help you generate evidence to use as leverage for additional compensation, promotion, and opportunities.

A regular valuation practice supports your market readiness. You can use WHO valuation outputs to produce value points for your resume, adjust your value proposition and pitch, and align with new and challenging opportunities either with your current company or elsewhere. Your value evolves as a result of the practice, and your advancement options are more confident and clearer due to reflection and assessment.

JANE T. AVATAR'S PROFESSIONAL DEVELOPMENT STORY – 5 YEARS LATER

Armed with a well-developed WHO Mindset, Jane T. Avatar, digital marketing specialist, negotiated two salary increases, served as lead on several high-profile projects, and received one unprompted salary increase based on her ability to align, articulate, and leverage value.

Within 18 months, and using the Weekly WHO Valuation Practice combined with several Comprehensive Valuation Checkups, Jane's valuable contributions elevated her from digital marketing specialist to a market research analyst role at UVW.

During her 3 years in the market research role, supported by a consistent WHO valuation practice, Jane became an expert at confidently negotiating new challenges and salary increases. She also developed a robust internal and external network. Jane leveraged smart work, valuation, and networking to make the move into her next role, business development director at GHI Inc.

Along the way, Jane T. Avatar initiated and strategically visioned her growth while carefully aligning work with the outputs and outcomes valued by UVW. She built a strong internal and external network, earned advocacy from others, and used continuous valuation to self-advocate.

Moving to GHI Inc. was a significant and strategic move for Jane. Recall from Chapter 8 Jane's interest in building a relationship with Mark, a contact from GHI. Mark was unresponsive to Jane's outreach efforts after an informational interview. Jane made the decision to let the relationship with Mark *lie fallow,* and she invested more time on other promising connections.

Once on the job with UVW, Jane reached out to Mark at GHI. She updated him on her progress and thanked him for the time he gave her while she was seeking internship opportunities. Mark responded immediately, letting Jane know he had been heavily involved in critical projects for GHI during their initial interactions and had been unable to respond to her post-informational interview messaging. He congratulated Jane on her professional progress and asked her to stay in touch. She did. And a mutually valued and reciprocal relationship developed between Mark and Jane. Years later, Mark informed Jane about the business development director role with GHI, and he served as her advocate throughout the application and hiring process.

Jane's career advancement journey will continue, supported by a healthy valuation mindset, powered by WHO Logic, and reinforced by outstanding networking skills, curiosity, and empathy.

Jane T. Avatar is a character. She represents a story of how taking control of the journey can advance a career. Please know there are many different variables that can impact career advancement. You may find yourself in need of change or new challenges, or you may need to make a lateral move to something completely different. Career trajectories are not necessarily vertically ascending. Sometimes the path meanders, for a multitude of reasons. There are even influences, sometimes out of your control, that make it challenging to thrive. Sometimes there just comes a moment when you feel you must go.

TIME TO GO

In my work, I am often asked questions such as when is it time for a change, time to move to a next level, time to leave a non-growth situation behind, time to obtain additional formal education? The answer is much easier if it's based in valuation and evidence. If you deploy a regular valuation practice, you will find your answers.

My advice is not to go if you haven't gathered the data to help you with this decision. Give yourself the gift of inquiry and valuation. A little WHO Logic can go a long way.

I also think it's important to share your journey. Try not to make the stay or go decision in isolation. Identify trusted individuals you can share, ideate, and strategize with in support of your career advancement.

CAREER MANAGEMENT PARTNERSHIPS & ACCOUNTABILITY

Career advancement planning is a strategic endeavor advantaged by collaboration and support. Regardless of career level or phase, find a career management accountability partner or form an accountability group. Lifelong career planning is not an assignment, nor is it a project at work for which you receive compensation. Accountability partnerships can support this incredibly important endeavor, if for no other reason than just keeping the career management topic fresh and active.

CHAPTER END & NEXT UP

So there you have it, tools to support your career advancement strategy. Carve out time for valuation. Take yourself to coffee or lunch regularly and stay true to reflection and assessment. It's an important part of career advancement. Give yourself permission to *WHOify*.

Next up you will find brief chapters promoting WHO Logic for companies and WHO Logic for life. See you there...

12

WHO Logic for Companies

Yes, you do want a *WHO Mindset* employee. Why? Very early on in their employment, a WHO Logic individual will align their work with the mission, values, strategic actions, and outcomes that define the company and business unit.

They will be engaged and productive. The WHO Mindset employee uses a smart work perspective along with valuation to prioritize and align their work. They know how to map and value their productivity. It's how they have been educated. If clear strategic initiatives and success metrics do not exist, they will help identify and create a guiding compass to ensure that value is created and outcomes are achieved.

From the perspective of assessment, WHO Logic is a full-circle evaluation tool that moves beyond measurement of **what** the person achieved and **how**. WHO Logic closes the loop by focusing on **outcomes**, the value-add aspect of work, in direct alignment with strategic targets articulated by the business unit and organization.

I suggest, if you haven't already, please make performance evaluations meaningful, evidence-based, and value-centered. Designing a WHO Logic performance evaluation practice could be a complementary and collaborative approach when working with a WHO Mindset employee.

Deploying WHO Logic at the time you interview a prospective employee and continuing the use of WHO from onboarding through regular performance evaluations creates a common language and mindset. Speaking a similar language—WHO Language—supports learning. The valuation concept is introduced, repetition and recall support the learning, and learning is deep and sticky by way of elevated practice.

It's so much easier to support growth, raises, and promotions if all parties seeking value find and speak a similar language. WHO has the potential to clarify and unify that language.

13

WHO Logic for Life

We have come to the end of our WHO Logic journey. I hope there are pieces from this work that resonate with you and provide support for your unique career advancement travels. For me, WHO truly is a mindset. It's a way of thinking that enriches exploration, investigation, reflection, and evaluation of... well, anything.

WHO helps you inquire, assess, and value, and it can keep you focused on the most relevant and important priorities in work and life. I like using WHO Logic for almost everything I do professionally and often for what I do personally.

I believe that valuation is one of the most important practices an individual can habituate. The practical and tactical samples and advice in this book are nimble. Use this information as you like. Adapt the examples and alter WHO valuation for your needs. Just be sure to incorporate some form of valuation in your work life.

Fundamentally and collectively, WHO Logic is about people. It takes people to create value. WHO? People, that's WHO. Yeah, I can't ever resist... I love the acronym.

So, here are my parting words.

→ Engage and collaborate in the value of the world around you.

→ Link your value to the stuff in life that is important to you.

→ Share WHO you are by confidently identifying, assessing, and articulating your value.

→ There is no one in the world that can better evaluate your value than you.

Happy Valuation.

WHO Logic – WHO Mindset.

APPENDIX

**RESUME VALUE POINT DISSECTION PRACTICE SETS –
FROM JANE T. AVATAR'S RESUME**

PRACTICE SET 1:

Before WHO Logic - Bullet Point:
- Managed social media for company.

After WHO Logic - Value Point:
- Built social media presence using coupons and time-sensitive campaigns, increased sales by 25% within 6 months of launch.

➡ ***WHO Logic Dissection:*** Built social media presence is the What; Using coupons and time-sensitive campaigns represents How the social media presence is developed; and the Outcome is increased sales by 25% within 6 months of launch.

➡ ***The value of How:*** The reader is informed that Jane T. Avatar has marketing skills. By applying WHO Logic, Jane offers specific evidence of important marketing skills based on her ability to use technology, coupons, and outreach campaigns.

➡ ***The value of Outcome(s):*** The reader (an employer) can see the outcome, increased sales by 25% within 6 months of launch. An employer can better predict Jane's ability to add value in the future and, because Jane has moved through the process of valuation, she can confidently speak to the value.

PRACTICE SET 2:

Before WHO Logic - Bullet Point:
- Filled in for supervisor as needed.

After WHO Logic - Value Point:
- Assumed leadership role during periodic manager absences and ensured uninterrupted store operations for business with $1.2M in annual sales.

➔ **WHO Logic Dissection:** Assumed leadership role is the What; Leadership during periodic absences represents How store operations are maintained; and the Outcome is uninterrupted store operations with the addition of the dollar amount in sales to provide scope.

➔ **The value of How:** The reader is informed that Jane can be trusted to take on leadership and a high level of responsibility, important professional skills.

➔ **The value of Outcome(s):** The reader (an employer) can predict Jane's ability to lead and responsibly manage significant projects and tasks. An employer can better predict Jane's ability to add value in the future and, because Jane has moved through the process of valuation, she can confidently speak to the value.